D1498657

THE NIX HOUSES

THE NIX HOUSES

Innovation and Style in Texas' Oldest Historic District

Roy R. Pachecano

THE
WATERCRESS
PRESS

San Antonio

2007

A *Watercress Press* book
from Geron & Associates
www.watercresspress.com

Book design:
Fishead Design Studio & Microgallery
www.fisheadproductions.com

ISBN-13: 978-0-934955-71-3
ISBN-10: 0-934955-71-9

Library of Congress Control Number: 2007921386

Manufactured in the United States of America

To Sophia, Arianna, and Alexei —
they add to the meaning 'a house houses memories.'

CONTENTS

ILLUSTRATIONS

ACKNOWLEDGEMENTS

Words cannot express my deepest gratitude and respect held for my father, Omar, who understood the importance of restoring the Nix Houses. He leaves a respectable mark on his native city which is a continuance of stewardship in the art of building that he inherited from his father's company, N. Pachecano & Sons Concrete Construction Company—a firm that built many foundations upon which generations of San Antonians have built their home.[1] And to my mother, Antonia, who always encouraged me to "be different, don't waste time, and get the job done."

My gratitude is extended to Patricia (Pat) Ezell who played an instrumental role in fact-gathering and assisted with great accuracy in collecting historical information that is the cornerstone of this book. If someone sneezed in Alamo Plaza in 1850, and it was recorded, Pat could find it. She also offered her critique on the subject matter which has greatly improved the content of the book. In addition to fact-finding, Pat offered critical insight that broadened the reach of the audience, and in so doing, extended the book to potential readers beyond preservationists.

My gratitude is extended to J. M. and Birdie Nix, Atlee B. Ayres, and W. B. Massey—the original development team—for leaving me a pair of houses to reposition; while they are not here today in a physical sense, they are strongly felt as a result of the multitude of details they left behind.

My gratitude goes also to some of the descendants of the Nix Family who assisted in the conveyance of firsthand family history: Helen "Suzie" Brooks Piña, great-granddaughter of Birdie Nix (Mrs. Piña's mother was Josephine Madison Nix), Christopher Ross and Kate Coiner Park, great-great-grandson and great-great-granddaughter respectively.

Thanks also go to Virginia Nicholas, Bruce MacDougal, and Félix D. Almaráz, Jr., Ph.D., for their guidance. Mrs. Nicholas—incoming president of the San Antonio Conservation Society at the time of publication—and Mr. MacDougal, the society's executive director, provided ample encouragement . . . meaning, they steered positive energy my direction in contrast to the well-known proclamations issued by the Society during any given public hearing before the city's historic commission which could send a developer's proposal back to the drawing boards, effectively tying up a project for months, years. Thanks to Dr. Almaráz, Distinguished Professor of Borderlands History at the University of Texas San Antonio, an authority on South Texas history, who was gracious enough to offer his historical perspective by way of his foreword for this volume.

I acknowledge Professor Emeritus James Robert Coote of the University of Texas Austin. Professor Coote's seminal work on Atlee

B. Ayres brought us together to share information. Mary Carolyn George, who in her own right is an architectural historian of great repute on architects who were Ayres' contemporaries, such as Alfred Giles, offered candid feedback. Without their encouragement and professionalism, our research at the Alexander Architectural Archives at the University of Texas Austin would have been protracted.

My thanks to colleagues at Columbia University who remain a wellspring of information—Janet Parks, Curator of the Drawings and Archives, and Avery Director Gerald Beasley. Avery Library is the world's best architectural library in which to conduct research and I thank the school for its access. Thanks to Jocelyn K. Wilk at the Columbia University Archives; the material at the university repository room dates back to the reign of King George II of England where one can trace not only the history of the school, but of the United States—an indispensable treasure. I was elated to discover Atlee B. Ayres had a connection to Columbia College by way of the Archive's office. Special heartfelt thanks to Michael P. Buckley, Director of the Real Estate Development Program at Columbia, who kindly provided both the Preface for this book and the squib for the dust jacket.

Thanks to Nancy Sparrow, guardian of the Alexander Architectural Archives at the University of Texas Austin. Without her stewardship, the Ayres collection would not be what it is: a marvelous assortment of architectural drawings.

My thanks to Ms. Linda Seckelson, Head of Reader Services at the renowned Thomas J. Watson Library of the Metropolitan

Museum of Art in New York. My thanks to Catherine Jenkins, Assistant Curator at the Department for Drawings and Prints at the Met who provided access to rare and wonderful trade catalogues for ornamental tile and the decorative arts.

Thanks to Ms. Gale Caskey Winkler, Ph.D., FASID, of LCA Associates who met with me at the Athenaeum in Philadelphia and was able to recreate a picture of the decorative art scene at the end of the nineteenth century.

A special thanks to Tom Shelton at the Institute of Texan Cultures (ITC). Mr. Shelton was very helpful and conscientious in providing the Ayres' account/ledger books for us. Had he never culled detailed information about the plumber, the electrician, the general contractor, and specialists who worked on the the Nix Houses, this information would not have been readily found (the accounting/ledger information contained in this book are not cata-logued at the ITC) and it took someone like Mr. Shelton, who remains trustworthy and interested in preserving Ayres materials, to fish out these rare facts.

I am grateful to the utility pole conversion team. These are the unsung heroes that helped turn around a small part of the public domain in King William: Chris and Ken at CPS, Donald and Joe at Time Warner, and Sarah at AT&T. This single phase of the restora-tion program did more to spark an awareness of our streetscape than the restoration of the dwellings themselves.[2]

I wish to thank two families: Carvajal and Bouquet. Specifically,

Alfonso (Al) Carvajal and Edna Rose Reed Bouquet, nonagenarians who benefited from their progenitors in inheritance of a pair of houses and managed to keep them intact over fifty-plus years as owner-occupied residences. (Remarkable, considering that the average American family today moves once every three to five years).

I'd like to recognize the men and women who became part of my corporate sphere of influence: bankers, lawyers, and advisors. Broadway Bank's Harvey Hartenstine, Jeannette Flores Westbrook, and Ken D. Herring. No real estate development project fraught with risk and unforeseen conditions is easy to underwrite. Together with Broadway Bank, we found a way. Thanks to local counsel Brian Maverick, Esq., who watches every detail with a cautious eye and keeps our legal guard defensible.

My thanks to Robert B. Knight, who has partnered with me on financial advisory assignments for banking clients on large real estate acquisitions and who has a keen eye for art in the medium of photography. It is not often you can have a meaningful conversation with someone who can switch back and forth from the analytical to creative sides of your brain. I enjoy his company and intellect.

My thanks to the San Antonio Convention and Visitor's Bureau whose location on South St. Mary's Street offered great city views of important works by Atlee B. Ayres. The Bureau provided timely shelter from the rain during a schedule-pressed photo shoot.

Finally, an offering of gratitude is given to the publisher of this book, Alice Geron of Watercress Press, known for her boutique style as publisher of South Texas histories. Finding the right publisher for the right book is the key to delivering the best story possible to the public. I'm grateful for Alice's contribution to this documentary.

These people, places, and institutions helped in the production of this book.

FOREWORD

People who leave their local environment to relocate in adjacent, yet distant, territory or even in a different continent, generally convey, besides food, clothing, books, and small paraphernalia, a figurative cultural handbag containing living memories and values which sustain them in their adjustment to alien surroundings. Before long, the newcomers transplant deep cultural roots in their new neighborhood that reflect commemorative swatches of the homeland from where they emigrated.

At various times in the history of San Antonio, visitors have called the local site a city of shadows, an old Spanish village, a sleepy cow-town by the railroad tracks, or a kaleidoscope of cultures (Hispanic, Mexican, Anglo-American, French, German, Irish, and later other hyphenated groups such as African-Americans, Poles, and Italians). By the mid-nineteenth century, San Antonio definitively possessed discernable characteristics of a kaleidoscope in passage. Between 1853 and 1859, city planners authorized private developers, in piecemeal fashion, to lay out streets in the historic King William District, just south of the central commercial corridor, on a land tract that previously had been designated *las labores de abajo* (the lower farmlands) of Mission San Antonio de Valero (later renowned as the Alamo).

In 1793, Spanish government officials began the process of secularizing the Franciscan missions, signifying that these frontier institutions of assimilation had fulfilled the purpose of their founding which was to convert the indigenous people into sedentary, productive, tax-paying, responsible residents of the community. Gradually the King William District encompassed most of Mission Valero's *labores de abajo*, the segment of land bordered by Alamo Street on the east and the San Antonio River on the west. Reportedly, Ernst Hermann Altgelt recommended the name for the principal thoroughfare—King William—in honor of Wilhelm I, King of Prussia (1861-1871), who personified the political movement that culminated in the nineteenth-century German Unification.

Following the turbulent years of the Civil War, Reconstruction, and the re-admission of Texas into the Union, San Antonio attracted a surge of immigration, migration, and investment capital that stimulated further development of the King William District. By 1877, the advent of the railroad enabled bankers, merchants, contractors, and architects in San Antonio to broaden their vision of what San Antonio might become. Specifically, the railroad provided the opportunity for architects and contractors to increase their inventory of construction materials that satisfied the emerging tastes for innovative designs in homes and commercial buildings.

By the last decade of the nineteenth century, the convergence of

railroad lines in San Antonio and the economic activity they generat-
ed further stimulated the development of adjacent streets in the King
William District (Alamo, Cedar, St. Mary's—formerly Garden—and
Pereida). King William Street, however, gained social prominence
because of the design, quality of construction, variety of building
materials, and the prestige of the architects and the proprietors whose
names became synonymous with the mansions in the neighborhood. J.
M. and Birdie Nix (proprietors) and Atlee B. Ayres (architect) typified
a younger generation of developers who collaborated in the construction of two homes at the corner of King William and East Johnson
streets that would set off their respective careers.

Roy R. Pachecano has composed a short documentary about a
development project that originated over a hundred years ago in
another era, in a particular place, and in a different society which is relevant today; the narrative reaches out to anyone who is interested in
learning about the architectural development of an historic neighborhood in San Antonio and offers hints at how to make these older
dwellings exceed today's green building standards. It is also an account
of the convergence of three individuals late in the nineteenth century:
J. M. and Birdie Nix, and Atlee B. Ayres.

The Nixes represent outsiders who influenced development in
San Antonio. They were born in Alabama before the end of the Civil
War. After Reconstruction they immigrated to Texas in search of
opportunities to succeed in business. Together they formed a formida-
ble force in early twentieth-century development in South Texas.

The other figure, Atlee Bernard Ayres, represents an outsider who influenced style in San Antonio as no other before him. Born on July 12, 1873, in Hillsboro, Ohio, he became an adopted San Antonian at an early age; the Ayres family moved to Houston, where they lived temporarily; in 1888 they migrated to San Antonio. At age seventeen, young Atlee traveled to New York to study at the Metropolitan School of Architecture—a program itself within the famous walls of the Metropolitan Museum of Art and in affiliation with Columbia College which sponsored lectures and provided library materials. The cooperative arrangement allowed students and faculty to tap the resources of both institutions. In addition to the regular curriculum at the Met, Ayres enrolled in night classes in drawing at the Art Students League, and, on Sundays, studied painting under the instruction of Frank Vincent Dumont. After graduation from the Met in 1894, Ayres traveled to Mexico where he spent almost two years before returning to San Antonio to launch a career. In his fledgling years as an architect, Ayres befriended the Nixes.

This documentary chronicles the first critical step in what would become an escalating staircase of successful architecture and development projects produced by the Nix and Ayres families in South Texas.

Félix D. Almaráz, Jr., Ph.D.
Peter T. Flawn Distinguished University
Professor of Borderlands History
The University of Texas at San Antonio

1. *Watercolor, 434 King William at East Johnson. (Roy Pachecano)*

2. *Watercolor, 432 King William facade. (Roy Pachecano)*

PREFACE

Historians and antique dealers share an inordinate interest in the provenance of objects—the threads of historical facts that tie the object to its place in time. For the antique dealers, the object's provenance proves the authenticity of a claim to the specific time, and the weave of additional stories collected proves the emotional value of the connections to the past. These are critical to the antique value of the object.

Houses too have rich stories to tell—and some have architectural quality to warrant a proof of legitimacy. Roy Pachecano has written such a weave of facts and additional stories told through two historic San Antonio houses—the remarkable collaboration between a pioneer Texas merchant and his designer. Pachecano convinces us to suspend judgement as in the cinema, and to place ourselves firmly in time with the original design and construction. Such a colleciton of facts and transmitted stories puts a significant coating of lives, economies, and cultures as an overlay to the architectural history of these structures.

Personalities create great architecture—typically driven by the combination of a moneyed client and a striving architect—enabled by the fortunes of a specific time and place. Many significant architectural structures survive multiple owners and varied economic circumstances to find themselves a focus of renewal and enhancement, as a new order recognizes the historic and emotional content and can celebrate the building's fine architectural framework.

All of these dynamics fuse together in this intriguing profile of the Nix Houses in the King William District of San Antonio. This book is a great read, with evocative historical facts and a wonderful story.

Michael P. Buckley
Director, MSc Real Estate Development Program
Columbia University

THE NIX HOUSES

3. *Watercolor, 432 King William courtyard. (Roy Pachecano)*

4. *Watercolor, 434 King William streetscape. (Roy Pachecano)*

INTRODUCTION

I f houses house memories, at what point does a dwelling transcend the materials and labor that built it? Can the business in the art of the deal be tamed and taken over by forces that transport our being? This book addresses these questions in a documentary format. From both a literal and figurative sense, the Nix Houses were a result of the transportation of material and ideas. Literally every part of the Nix Houses came from somewhere else—facts that were lost to time but recovered with hard-nosed research.

This is essentially a short story about a real estate development deal that occurred in a different society with astounding relevance for the future. It is an essay that documents the innovative strategies and elements of risk-taking that, while veiled as a business-driven proposition, flowered into a private development that has withstood the test of time, markets, fashion, and lifestyles. It can serve as a model that explores the delicate balance of making a deal and place-making.

The collection of this text and concomitant research began by accident. When I was informed by Pat Ezell she had discovered that the Nix Houses were designed by Atlee B. Ayres in 1899, you could have knocked us down with a feather. Ayres, of course, was a prominent architect in South Texas. Coincidentally, at just about this time I was learning about Ayres from Robert James Coote's seminal book entitled *The Eclectic Odyssey of Atlee B. Ayres, Architect.* The importance of the real estate deal in 2006, not only in terms of its repositioned structure, but the added value and historical contribution to the history of downtown San Antonio grew significantly. As it turned out, we discovered it was Ayres' first work as well as the Nix family's first deal—both entities whose career paths in designing and erecting monumental edifices in South Texas have their starting point with this project. As if by providence, I would discover numerous parallels from the original project to my current re-development project.

Naturally, questions arose from these initial findings such as, "What are New England houses doing in South Texas? Why two houses instead of one? How was the first deal financed? Why so much fuss over small details like tile and fireplace mantels?" When comparing the relative small magnitude of the event this book chronicles to the larger looming questions of life, I felt in writing and researching much like an astrologer peering into the tiniest bits of matter and pondering the infinity of the universe. It is the smallest things that often hold the key to the grander concepts.

Perhaps more important were the underlining business inquiries such as: How to finance a bold intervention? Can you fuse history with high-technology? And, at its core, simply: Can you remake a classic? In an effort to address these questions, this book documents the restoration of these unique homes and was written in such a way as to effortlessly be absorbed by professionals and non-professionals alike. One can read this pocket book in one sitting, or return to it at your own leisure.

By the time I was invited to speak at the American Institute of Architect's 2007 national convention in San Antonio to deliver a seminar entitled, "Integrating Green Design with Historic Preservation," (from a developer's perspective), the research and manuscript had achieved book form. Historic preservation is usually not mentioned in the same sentence with sustainable, green design, let alone green luxury residences. I seek to advance the practical notions of applying these two disciplines which have often been viewed as separate elements in the discourse of design and construction.

As a developer mostly concerned with expenditure, time value of money, IRR (Internal Rate of Return), Yield on Cost, ROI (Return on Investment), and the delivery of a product to the marketplace, the writing of this short story compliments my professional work. It follows a return to San Antonio after some thirty years, with almost twenty having been spent in New York City. If history is prologue, I have indulged in the discovery of how another developer at another career crossroads similarly dealt with the deployment of capital, engaging a team composed of an architect and contractor who endeavored to create understatedly elegant, habitable spaces.

Developers are often assailed for overlooking the essence of refined living at the expense of a quick return. This volume does not primarily focus on the speed-to-market strategy surrounding a development project. Rather, its broader, higher aim is to pause and revisit a central theme of real property value: why we as a society feel insouciantly toward our homes and choose to discard, throw away, and replace rather than hold onto, keep, and restore. There is no question it is more difficult to engage in restoration than to build a ground-up new building. This challenge, and those who took up the same challenge decades before my arrival in King William, served as inspiration and a yardstick for substantive progress.

Research was undertaken in the San Antonio Public Library, Texana-Genealogy Department, the San Antonio Conservation Society Library, the San Antonio Genealogical and Historical Society Library, the Library at the Institute of Texan Cultures-University of Texas at San Antonio, the Bexar County Courthouse Deed Records Archives, the Alexander Architectural Archives of the University of Texas-Austin, the Columbia University Archives, Avery Architectural and Fine Arts Library of Columbia University, the Thomas J. Watson Library, the Department for Drawings and Prints at the Metropolitan Museum of Art in New York City, and the Collections Library at the Athenaeum in Philadelphia. Where noted, research on land and property transfers was performed by direct inquiries at the municipal archives and records offices in Bexar County, Texas. This research was supplemented with further investigation into written articles, books, newspapers, and trade publications as well as online, internet databases. Finally, direct interviews were conducted with descendants of the Nix family, the content of which was incorporated into this paper.

This book on the Nix Houses is intended to achieve the primary objective of preserving and cataloging two of Texas' historically and architecturally significant residences. The research substantiated herein reinforces an interpretative essay that weaves the architectural significance with other findings such as the social, economic, and political histories that were contemporaneous with the creation of the Nix Houses.

I. CONTEXT AND CITY

The official name given by the Texas Historical Commission for 434 King William is "J. M. and Birdie Nix House," in honor of Mr. Joseph Madison (Joseph Madison Napoleon Bonaparte Nix) and Mrs. Birdie Lanier Nix. The sister house next door, located at 432 King William, has not been designated at the time this publication goes to press. The two dwellings, hereinafter referred to as 432 and 434 or individually mentioned, are located in the downtown King William Historic District of San Antonio. This gracious block has long been recognized for its original and distinctive character that makes it the "Fifth Avenue" of Texas' oldest inner-city urban community. In the mid-to-late 19th century, this precinct was to become the home to many influential German immigrants and first generation European-Texans. This area became widely known as a place of distinction in South Texas because of the preponderance of German merchants, tradesmen, bankers, doctors, lawyers, and politicians who later became influential in the post-Civil War development of San Antonio.[3]

The Nix Houses are located at the key intersection of King William and East Johnson streets.[4] The houses sit diagonally across the street from the monumental home of Edward and Joanna Steves, known as 509 King William and currently operating as "The Steves Homestead Museum."[5] The magnificent Steves' residence was the first house built on King William in 1867 by Ernst Altgelt, who gave the street the name "King William."[6 7 8]

The King William Historic District was on the outskirts of San Antonio at the time the land was surveyed.[9] It is referenced as a plat of town lots surveyed in 1859 for N. A. Mitchell and drawn by G. Freisleben, City Surveyor. Thus the King William Area streets were surveyed between the years of 1853 and 1859 and became a part of the City of San Antonio.[10 11] This newly surveyed area represented a succession of rapid growth periods when the old city of San Antonio began to grow outside its inner-European core. Today, this precinct of the city is undeniably a part of the downtown urban experience of San Antonio, which has remained Texas' "Cradle of Independence" (the Alamo is only one mile away).

Originally, this land comprised a portion of the *labor de abajo*, or "lower labor" assigned as farm land to the San Antonio de Valero Mission, known as the Alamo. After the mission was secularized in 1793, the lower farmland was divided into equal tracts for the fourteen Indian families in the area.[12] Deed records indicate numerous landowners held the property, or greater swatches, tracts, or "suertes" of the land, until it was subdivided. Original grantees such as Vicente Amador, who had the duty of assigning these grants in 1793, and Pedro Huizar, who was the surveyor, between them were given the greater

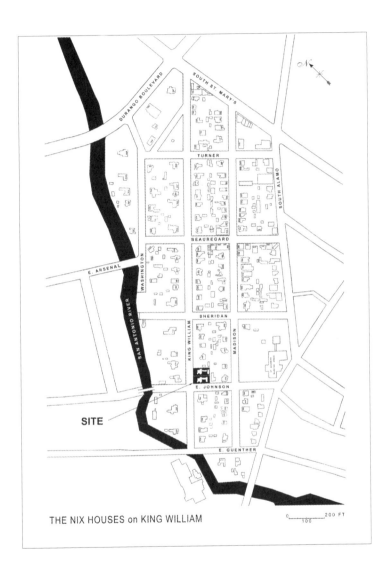

5. *Map, King William Area.* (*Roy Pachecano*)

6. *Koch, Augustus, "Bird's Eye View of San Antonio Bexar County, Texas 1886, Looking East." Toned lithograph, 28 x 37 in. Note the location of the Nix Houses ("Site") in relation to the Alamo. (Lithographer unknown)*

part of what is known today as the King William area. Over the next three decades, the original grantees began to sell their property so that by 1823 most of it was purchased to form large holdings. These later owners sold their tracts to land developers.[13]

Vicente Amador sold his "suerte" in 1813 to Manuel Barrera for $300; he in turn sold it to Juan McMullen in 1832 for $160. McMullen sold it in 1844 to Thomas J. Devine[14] for $600. In 1853, when Devine sold some of his land to Catherine Elder, it is described as a tract of land "adjoining the City of San Antonio." By 1863, deed transfer for a part of this tract is referred to as "certain city lots in the City of San Antonio" and describes them by block and number.[15]

In 1878, Thomas J. Devine sold the two parcels of land at 432 and 434 King William to Charles C. Cresson and Adelia (Van Derlip) Cresson. The land was described as "lying between Guenther's upper and lower mills, Lots 16, 17, & 18, Block #5," according to the original plat of surveys made by G. Freisleben. A purchase price of $100 was paid initially with a sum of $848 to follow within 18 months.[16] [17] Charles and Adelia sold Lots 17 & 18, Block 5, New City Block (NCB) #746 to J. M. and Birdie L. Nix in 1899 for the sum of $2,500.[18] These lots or parcels, purchased by J. M. and Birdie Nix in 1899, are the earliest known property acquisitions in San Antonio by the Nix family who were to become a dynamic husband-and-wife real estate development team.[19] [20]

II. THE NIX FAMILY

When J. M. and Birdie Nix[21], formerly of Alabama, arrived in San Antonio from Tennessee in the early 1890's, J. M. went into the furniture business as the manager for Stelson Furniture Company on East Houston Street. By 1901 he was a sales manager for the Stowers Furniture Company and by 1903 he was associated with B. J. Wilkinson at the Nix Furniture Company at 218 West Houston Street.[22] J. M. also was one of the first merchants to offer individuals an opportunity to purchase goods on an installment plan. This was begun in his joint business venture with J. T. Nored as the N & N Installment Company.[23]

Birdie Nix was in the real estate business and was known to be a very astute and independent businesswoman. She was listed as B. L. Nix at the same business address as J. M. In 1896, J. M. and Birdie's residence was listed as 315 San Pedro Avenue. In 1899, their residence was listed as 525 Madison Street.[24] By 1900, J. M., Birdie and their young son, Joe Lanier Nix, were living at 432 King William. J. M.'s occupation was "Furniture Merchant."[25] In 1910 they were living at 470 Baltimore Avenue on the northern side of downtown.[26] J. M. 's occupation during this time was listed as "Railroad Promoter." Apparently, J. M. was a "front man" for the St. Louis & Brownsville Railroad, now the Missouri Pacific, to acquire right of way for the tracks.[27] By 1920 J. M. and Birdie had settled at the Lanier Hotel at 207 East Travis as they are living there both in the 1920 and 1930 census reports. J. M. was the hotel proprietor.[28] The Lanier Hotel later became the White Plaza Hotel which the Nix team helped to develop. They also lived in the penthouse of the Majestic Building; J. M. was involved in the development because they owned the land which he leased to the Majestic partnership. He was involved in setting up amusement and vaudeville houses, so popular in this time period, and befriended celebrities in the performing arts.[29]

It is speculated that J. M. and Birdie Nix went into the hotel business due to the scarcity of available rooms for those visiting the city. In 1901 there were only ten hotels advertising in the daily newspaper, the *San Antonio Daily Express*. In 1907 a feature article in the paper proclaimed that more hotels were needed in San Antonio. C. B. Mullaly advocated for more hotels in a speech before the Business Men's Club. He said that people were being turned away day and night due to lack of hotel room availability and that "High living has become a fine art, no one is going to leave a palatial residence to be housed like a piece of baggage in a hotel simply because of the delightful climate of San Antonio."[30]

The J. M. and Birdie team were to be intimately involved in the development and ownership of several deals: The Medical Arts Building—the soaring Gothic-inspired skyscraper that graces the northern edge of Alamo Plaza—the Majestic Theater facing the Gunter Hotel on Houston Street, the Lanier-White Plaza Hotel, the Nueces Hotel in Corpus Christi, the El Jardín and the Capitol Theatre in Brownsville, the Madison Hotel in Harlingen, and the Raleigh Hotel in Waco.[31] As discussed later, a large portion of what is now the South Texas Medical Center and Oak Hills Country Club was the Nix Dairy Farm. J. M. "brokered" the sale of what is now the San Antonio Water System from George W. Brackenridge to the city.[32]

J. M. Nix was active in both civic and social affairs of his adopted city, being a member of the Knights of Pythias, the Elks, a member of the Chamber of Commerce, and a member of the fraternity D.K.E.[33] These activities, no doubt, facilitated his contacts with key businessmen in the city.

Before it was over, the building legacy J. M. and Birdie Nix left behind was nothing short of astounding in San Antonio. Within three decades, the duo assembled a portfolio of urban edifices they helped develop that remain iconic landmarks in San Antonio and throughout South Texas. From low-lying elegant houses to hotels, theaters, and towering skyscrapers, the Nix family legacy is hinted at in the following obituary for J. M. Nix, dated June 1, 1932:

NIX SERVICES HERE WEDNESDAY
Hotel Man Was Stricken While in Brownsville

Funeral services for J. M. Nix, 65, hotel owner and real estate operator, who died in Brownsville Monday night following a paralytic stroke will be held Wednesday afternoon.

The body will arrive here Wednesday from Brownsville, accompanied by his son, Joe. L. Nix, who left for Brownsville Monday night upon receipt of his father's death, and his widow, who was with him at the time.

Nix, the owner of the Lanier Hotel here and builder of the Nix Professional Building, was taken ill in the lobby at the El Jardin Hotel in Brownsville, of which he is the principal stockholder, and died an hour and a half later.

Rt. Rev. William T. Capers, bishop of the Episcopal Diocese of West Texas, will conduct the services. Pallbearers will be E. J. Roe, Robert C. Smith, Richard Gill, Jack De Forest, Dick O. Terrell and Raymond Woodward.

Nix had been in ill health for several months and went to Brownsville three weeks ago with his wife to rest at the El Jardin Hotel, which he built about five years ago in cooperation with a group of Brownsville citizens.

Since he came to San Antonio from Tennessee 36 years ago, Nix had been prominent in hotel and real estate circles here and in other Texas cities. He formerly managed a furniture store and later operated a theater on the present site of the Majestic Theater, which he leased for the erection of the theater. He erected the 22-story Nix Professional Building which was completed last fall at a cost of more than $1,000,000.

Surviving besides his widow and son, are a sister, Miss Ella G. Nix, two half-brothers, Joe J. and R. F. Nix, and two granddaughters.[34]

Surely this legacy is felt nowhere stronger than in San Antonio where the three most recognizable urban buildings are a testament to the planning and development skills of the Nix family at the opening of the twentieth century: the Nix Professional Building (mostly referred to and also known as "the Nix Hospital")[35], the Medical Arts Building (now the Emily Morgan Hotel), and the Majestic Theater.

When the Nixes teamed up with Atlee B. Ayres for his first commission, much was in store for the development team and San Antonio was going to be the prime beneficiary. This first small commission was needed fuel to advance a predestined trajectory for the architect. In no less than twenty years from his start with the Nix Houses, Ayres would leave a string of monuments culminating with the much-loved Smith-Young Tower skyscraper which gracefully overlooks downtown San Antonio.[36] While other structures have come along since the 1930s which have been built higher, the Smith-Young Tower has never seemed to lose its ground nor be overtaken.

Like all great architects, we see Ayres extending his own vision into something more than self-aggrandizement. He had an ability to ignite enthusiasm for unbuilt work and kindle his private fire into a collective, corporate blaze. It is this type of vision that brought Ayres to the forefront of public awareness while he was still very young; by 1912 Ayres' visibility was rising with his appointment by San Antonio Mayor Augustus H. Jones as the chairman of the newly created City Plan Committee whose main charge was the adoption of a city plan that addressed the beautification of the river in San Antonio's downtown precinct. Embracing "City Beautiful" reforms—a national movement that combined civic and environmental activism with political reform to improve the public domain and thereby its citizenry, producing a positive economic effect—Ayres' river beautification plans became a priority nearly two decades before the now famous Robert Hugman became known as the architect of the Riverwalk—a river that is unquestionably San Antonio's urban gift and life-blood of the city.[v]

While the Nix Houses are not of the same genre as the monumental downtown structures, taken together, the twin dwellings of 432 and 434 serve as a harbinger for the Nix team who showed, early on, a sensitivity to scale, proportion, and elegance. Such attention to style is clearly evident in the designs of these King William residences by Ayres. Birdie Nix had assertive, yet subtle, influence over Ayres to acknowledge the surrounding Steves' family mansions built a decade earlier. The Nix Houses were not loyal to the idiosyncrasies of the region but their silhouettes sought to make a New Englander feel at home in South Texas. The result is an urban ensemble appropriately scaled and offering more than the developers could have expected.

Through the use of verandas and high-pitched roof lines, the scale of the modest residences ascended to match in height the stone villas facing the other three corners of the intersection. The Nix Houses are an example of "mirroring" in scale and proportion the adjacent, larger dwellings which sat on two- and three-lot parcels, making the much smaller single lot the Nix Houses occupied feel as grand

7. *Photograph, Smith-Young Tower. (Robert Knight)*

8. Photograph: Medical Arts Center, now the Emily Morgan Hotel.
(Robert Knight)

9. *Photograph: The Nix Hospital. (Robert Knight)*

and spacious as their neighbors. Thus, the effective deployment of site planning and the astute manipulation of economy of scale created cost effective elegant homes at the time of their design and construction.

III. FINANCING THE DEAL

With legal control of the surveyed King William lots by early fall 1899, J. M. and Birdie Nix set out to develop these two parcels, and with it, planted the seeds of real estate development that would alter the skyline of San Antonio. What they lacked to get into the real estate game was development capital. For this, they turned to the local capital markets as well as carefully negotiated seller-financing. Such deal-making was wholly within the Nix's business capacity, having successfully created innovative business strategies in the past. Now, they turned their attention to something much more substantial: acquiring land and building on it. The Nixes were in a good position to leverage their assets to greater real estate deals, leaving behind the furniture installment business.

But where to start acquiring land? J. M. relied on information he obtained from his railroad contacts.

The arrival of the railroad in 1877 was significant: It signaled the expansion of San Antonio's regional economy which made real estate holdings near these lines more valuable.[8] Such was this significance that the regulation of railroads (and the cottage industries that sprang from it) became the main issue in Texas politics during the Gilded Age

(1876-1900).[39] Drawing from his experience as a railroad promoter, J. M. Nix would have known of the plans of railroad companies to build three passenger railroad stations near downtown.[40] The new enclave of King William must have fit J. M. and Birdie Nix's market study profile; the parcels were located very close to two of San Antonio's main passenger train stations: the 1903 Sunset Depot, named by the Southern Pacific Railroad, and the 1908 International & Great Northern Railroad Depot, or IG&N, each approximately one mile from the parcels on King William.[41] A short time later, the Missouri-Kansas-Texas Railroad, known as the MKT or "The Katy" that had been using the Sunset Depot, established its own magnificent depot on Durango Street between South Flores and South St. Mary's streets, a site now occupied by the La Quinta Inn and Suites Hotel.[42]

The expansion of lumber companies and railroads also brought incentives for innovation. Contrary to misrepresented portraits of the South, lumber and railroad companies combined their efforts with local and federal governments to create a strong technological community.[43] In San Antonio, the long-established trade route as an East-West junction was fortified with renewed capital in the late 1800s. The city's historic North-South trade route with Mexico and Latin America was only temporarily hampered by war and revolution. But it too was revived so that by the late 1920s, the city was a bustling East-West and North-South junction. Beginning in the mid-1870s, new products were arriving by railroad from both coasts of the United States.

The development of the Nix property would reflect late-nineteenth century real estate acquisition techniques. The acquisition was financed by a private lender, the seller, with terms more stringent than we might find today in the commercial capital markets. Although privately financed, the players involved in this deal understood the emerging trends of finance and how to leverage the transaction. Structured debt and equity as we know it today for small scale real estate procurement in the United States was an area of finance that did not fully exist during the late 1890s but can best be described as an emerging area of finance triggered by tremendous economic, social, political, and cultural change.[44]

The US government's involvement with the secondary mortgage market (a specialized area where mortgage originators such as mortgage banking companies could sell mortgages and resupply capital with which new loans could be created) did not exist at this time and was not formally established until 1916 with the first farmer's credit program. It was not until the mid-twentieth century when the Federal Housing Administration and the Veterans Administration loan guarantee programs were created that this area of finance finally begins to mature.[45] This trend was heading towards the development of specialized credit markets where assets could be bought and sold on the basis of a future stream of income; the new credit instruments were considered titles to property.[46] As it related to the Nixes in the financing of their first deal, a change in how the federal courts viewed the essential nature of property directly affected their acquisition; that is, the courts linked not only the material substance of the assets but also the probable expectancy of future income from use of those assets.

Twenty-five years after the Civil War, the banking industry, firm-ly seated in the Northeast, had fueled development in many cities and towns in the South and Southwest United States. San Antonio came out of the War Between the States unscathed, unlike cities such as Atlanta which required much reconstruction effort. By the 1890s, San Antonio's population had grown to just under 40,000 and was ideally suited for post-reconstruction development not associated with rebuilding.

Investor loans for speculative housing deals could be found but with much shorter maturity periods and higher equity terms com-pared to today's conventional standards. Interest rates, much less reg-ulated amongst private lenders in 1899, could be found in the vicinity of 8-9%, depending on the source of funding. What is more impor-tant, however, was the fact that it was more common in the late 1890s to make an equity contribution exceeding today's nominal 10% down payment, effectively allowing real estate development to be controlled by the moneyed few. The Nix's 7% interest on the construction note was a good deal brought about by their skill in negotiating the terms. By comparison, at the time the deal was negotiated, the prime six-month commercial paper traded on the open market in December 1899 was listed at 7.38%.[47]

To investors, the prospects seemed limitless as San Antonio and Bexar County were experiencing their first major modern boom. There had been good trade years following the founding of the city by the

Spanish in 1716 but that period was nothing compared to San Antonio's expansion from the 1890s to the late 1920s that would change the character of life in Bexar County. During these three decades, the manufacturing and agricultural sectors grew rapidly. The 1890 US Census revealed the county's population was spiraling upward; between 1870 and 1920 San Antonio grew to 161,000 people, making it Texas's largest city.[48] This growth is in sharp contrast to figures from 1870 when the population has just exceeded 12,000.[49] The number of farms more than doubled to sustain the growing population—up to more than 3,200 with some 800,000 acres devoted to agriculture. And while Bexar County has never been considered a significant oil center, there was a steady increase in petroleum production after the late 1880s when oil was discovered in what was then known as the world's largest shallow oil field which ran from Somerset to present-day Brooks City-Base on the county's south side all the way to Pleasanton.[50 51] Before the stock market crash of 1929 and the following Great Depression of the 1930s, San Antonio would remain Texas' largest city with a population estimated at 225,000 by 1925.[52 53]

Economic news found in a period trade publication would likely have been provided to them by Ayres and understood by the Nixes as developers: "According to reports gathered from State Authorities, land is increasing in value in nearly all of the Western States, especially along or near lines of railroads."[54 55] It was the western-trade regional economy which provided the context where capital was invested in the city.

To start off their real estate careers as developers, J. M. and Birdie signed private promissory notes for the parcels on King William. When completed, they sold each property separately at different times spanning over a decade. Since the Nixes occupied the house at 432 King William, this financial study concentrates on the rental property at 434 King William. The historical information which follows chronicles how these private dealings became manifest.

When the Cressons sold the two lots to J. M. and Birdie for $2,500, eighteen-hundred dollars was paid in cash and two promissory notes were signed in the amount of $350 each at 8% interest per annum, payable semi-annually; Note 1 was due on or before one year after date of transaction, Note 2 due on or before two years after date of transaction. There was a vendor's lien retained on the property. These notes were paid off on December 20, 1899, and the vendor's lien was released. So, before New Year's Day 1900, the land under the houses was paid off. On the same December 20, 1899, W. B. Massey assigned his lien of $4,700 for the construction of the two houses to D. Hirsch to be paid in six months. Hirsch, as well as those that followed him until the Nixes were no longer involved, was essentially acting as a private banker trading paper.

With the plumber, Strohmeyer, owed $300 ($155 was paid on his contract), on March 24, 1900, (nine days after the construction completion deadline of March 15, 1900) Birdie Lanier Nix restructured the debt with D. Hirsch and referenced the $300 note to R. Strohmeyer due six months from said date that the original note was transferred to D. Hirsch. Perhaps due to the slow initial signing on of renters, Birdie Nix was "desirous of extending time of maturity." This suggests the Nixes were seeking an extension to pay off in a systematic timetable: "Payable: $500 due on Dec. 30, 1900, 1,000 due on Dec. 30, 1901, $1,000 due on Dec. 30, 1902, $1,000 due on Dec. 30, 1903 and $1,500 due on Dec. 30, 1904. 7% interest payable semi-annually, June & December in U.S. GOLD COIN."[6] The complicated history of deed transfers is provided as a summation of lien transfers and placed in the reference section at the rear of this book for further reading.[7]

To underwrite their first, ground-up real estate deal, the Nixes needed positive cash flow in an effort to pay off the construction note which represented more than quadruple the debt on the land. To accomplish this they rented the house next door as a "single family residence" to young professionals while they simultaneously took up residence at 432 King William.[8] Housing was scarce as apartment complexes did not yet dot the landscape, thereby necessitating that citizens rent rooms in local boarding houses, or, as the Nixes innovatively offered, a room with a view in a swank new house near places of professional employment.

At the time the Nixes sat down and wrote the math to make the deal work at these two parcels, they used a linear method of addition and subtraction to calculate their return on investment. Today, such simple "back of envelope" arithmetic is not customarily used for underwriting. To bring the financial analysis up-to-date, a simple Excel worksheet can create a financial proforma that illustrates the cash flow of the deal. For purposes of study, we have simplified the many variables in constructing a proforma for an operating cash-flow property and assumed the Nixes rented the four rooms available at 434 King William for an estimated $20 per month for each room—a conservative figure according to the prevailing market conditions at the time. Room rents varied from $1.00 to $1.50 per day to $30 per month depending on the location. In some areas of town, 5-room cottages rented for $35.00 per month. It is likely the King William area brought higher rents due to the proximity to the downtown area and the ambience of the neighborhood.[59]

While J. M. and Birdie would not have had access to today's computer software or even hand-held calculators, we have endeavored to recreate the cash flow engine they contemplated in 1899. What is revealed in the financial analysis is that the Nixes were very successful at leveraging their cash flow and that these twin houses became the Nix's launching pad for future, larger deals. With their equity position at $1,800, and a sale to Mary Gleason (see below) with a combined value of at least $7,000 ($5,000 included the land swap), the unleveraged yield on cost was over 200%. The computer model compared the estimated 1907 valuation with today's capitalization rate technique and revealed the leveraged return was likely worth more (the net sales proceeds was projected to be over $8,000 in 1907 using a 10% cap rate).[60]

With the land secured under the houses, a restructured construction note was essentially a move to refinance by the Nixes to a debt structure that might resemble today's 5-year note. The Nix's move into

432 and setting up 434 as a cash flow vehicle allowed them to live in their own development. The remaining $4,700 construction note got passed around as though traded as paper through deed transfers until the Nixes finally deeded over the property in 1907 to Mary Beall Gleason, a strong female from West Texas engaged in real estate like Birdie; the two must have seen themselves as equals. By 1907, the Nixes had accumulated $7,200 in rents and were in a position to leverage their rental property for larger deals.[61][62]

As a last note to this section, there is a remarkable side story. The many physicians, surgeons, nurses, and medical care experts who have been drawn to San Antonio do not realize that the twin houses in King William helped give birth to the medical industry in San Antonio in profound ways. It was the same Mary Gleason who traded the Nix House at 434 for undeveloped land that enabled the Nixes to start their venture in land speculation and dairy farming. The acreage that was used to establish the Nix landholding was part of the 200-acre tract which was subsequently sold to the State of Texas by the Five Oaks, Inc., group of developers to build a medical school and health science center. Today, the University of Texas Health Science Center in San Antonio is a world-renowned educational, research, and treatment center where internationally distinguished researchers seek cures for cancer and other diseases.[63][64][65] J. M. and Birdie's capital strength in real estate would not have not been realized if the Nix Houses had not been built. Because of their success, they were able to secure land which blossomed into a significant industry for San

Antonio. Thus, the financial returns for the Nix's first small scale real estate development resulted in a windfall for the Nix family as well as for the city at large.

IV. BUILDING THE NIX HOUSES

With the sale of the lots by the Cressons to the J. M./Birdie team in September 1899, much of the planning for building was already underway and within several months the twin houses at 432 and 434 King William were constructed.

The last days of December 1899 were cool and crisp in San Antonio.[66] It was likely scented with a hint of pine nuts mixed with the aroma of burning mesquite, pecan, and cedar along the stately row of mansions on King William. By December, the Nix duo forged head-long into the speculative building of high-end residential property. With legal control of the last vacant parcels at the corner of King William and East Johnson, and with architectural drawings in hand, the dynamic duo put forth a breathtaking question to the builder, W. B. Massey: Can you build two homes in keeping with the surrounding scale of mansions and fabricate them with select materials, fashionable design features, and complete them in two and a half months? Not to be outdone by the upstart team, the answer was apparently "yes."

On the afternoon of December 30, 1899, the Nix team contract-ed with W. B. Massey to build two, two-story frame buildings, fences, and outhouses in keeping with the drawings as prepared by the architect. As fate would have it, the architect selected was Atlee B. Ayres—an unknown and untested, young, energetic, and outgoing professional eager to start his first significant residential commission in San Antonio.

Ayres, who had studied at the newly formed School of Architecture at the Metropolitan Museum of Art (the Met) in New York City in 1892-1894, was fresh out of school. He returned briefly to San Antonio in 1896 prior to accepting a position in Mexico City with George Cook, a British architect. Ayres returned to San Antonio after one and a half years in Mexico and worked for a brief time with architects Alfred Beckman and Percy Knight before associating himself with C. A. Coughlin, another New York City architect practicing in San Antonio. In 1899, Coughlin went into partnership with Ayres but the business relationship only lasted a year owing to the death of Coughlin; this has led to the speculation that Ayres was attracted to associating himself with Coughlin because of the man's well-seasoned name and the experience and legitimacy it afforded.[67][68] The Nix Houses represent Ayres' earliest explorations in the colonial revival style and set the foundation for a career in high-end residential design which would become his *métier*.[69]

At a time when schools of architecture were neither numerous nor commonplace, Ayres found in New York a feast to the eyes of an aspiring apprentice. Ayres earliest works, in contrast to his work later in life, was heavily influenced by the simple free-classic form of the Colonial Revival style abundantly found in New York and New

10. *Portrait, J. M. Nix. (Nix Health Care System)*

11. *Portrait, Birdie Lanier Nix. (Kate Coiner Park)*

12. *Portrait, Atlee B. Ayres. (Institute of Texan Cultures)*

England.[70] The Nix Houses represent Ayres' earliest explorations in the Colonial Revival style.

Ayres was heavily influenced by the teachings on style at the Met and Columbia College. It was with reverence the word "style" entered into the vocabulary of apprentice-architects. The word is derived from the Latin *stilus*, a small pointed metal instrument used in writing and engraving. Its modern-day link and association to the word's image and appearance stems from the ancient use of a stilus intended to impress (physically) and influence (figuratively) the moral and intellectual aspirations of the literary artist. At the time Ayres was studying in New York, these aspirations in the field of architecture were based on: purity, propriety, precision, clearness, naturalness, and appropriateness—elements tied to the philosophy of John Ruskin and Gottfried Semper—the architectural intelligentsia of the time imported from Europe and brought fresh to the style-thirsty New York academic circles.[71]

Ayres would find his exploration of style further enhanced by the association of two of New York's most well-known institutions. At a meeting of the trustees held on the 7th day of December, 1891, the president of Columbia College laid before the board a communication dated December 5, 1891, addressed to President Seth Low, outlining the privileges to be granted to Columbia College by the Metropolitan Museum of Art. The letter acknowledged numerous matters such as admission to the museum, lectures delivered before objects, permission to sketch, draw, and the furnishing of a lecture room to seat 500

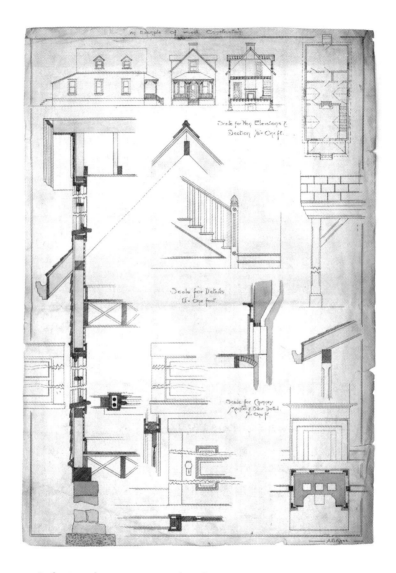

13. *Study of wood frame construction by Atlee B. Ayres. Drawn while Ayres studied at the Met in New York, 1892. Image at left illustrates balloon framing technique from foundation to upper levels. Firebox, overmantel, newel post, and window/door details perfectly match details found at the Nix Houses in San Antonio. (Alexander Architectural Archive, University of Texas, Austin)*

people if the college would agree to give public lectures.

Thus, two quintessential New York institutions resolved to collaborate in education through course exchanges on art and architecture to be delivered at the Metropolitan Museum of Art. This finding was confirmed at both institutions.[72][73][74] Ayres was personally introduced to Columbia's first dean of architecture, William Ware, by letter dated May 1, 1893, from Professor Seth Temple of the Met.[75][76]

Now grounded in design theory, it was time for Ayres to test his construction know-how. He offered his ability to produce a set of working drawings that answered the developer's call for innovative design invigorated with a high degree of finesse and style—so long as it fit within the developer's construction timetable.

The Nix contract typified construction agreements of the nineteenth century where the architect held a much broader role in the overall execution of construction. The architect, after all, had prepared his own set of drawings and could determine many aspects of the cost and engineering. Notwithstanding this, hiring an architect at that time was still not the norm—it was a luxury usually reserved for the wealthy patrons. When an owner/client did hire an architect, he relied on the architect for his knowledge of how buildings were constructed. The main reason why an owner/client in the nineteenth century did not typically retain an architect is because he simply didn't have to. The legal definition of the practice of architecture as we understand it today was not widely known nor were the numerous mandatory state licensing requirements codified in the United States; there was, in essence, a blurring between architect and builder which epitomized the term *master-builder.*[77]

Beginning shortly after the turn of the twentieth century, the fundamental relationship between design and construction began to change. The architect would slowly lose his place as the master-builder as construction became more specialized and the architectural profession, as a whole, was subject to perceived weaknesses and inefficiencies in the traditional construction process. Designers were faulted because of their casual attitude toward costs, their inability to predict costs (the basis of all financial modeling), and their ignorance of the labor and materials market, as well as costs of employing construction techniques.[78]

The Nix team was looking to Ayres to control and motivate the contractor into high gear. The work was to be completed by March 15, 1900, or the builder team would forfeit $5.00 per day for each day in default. Compared to today's penalty clauses found in owner-contractor and owner-architect agreements, the grounds for delay appear weighted heavily in favor of the owner as the contract further stated: "Any delay of unreasonable time in the opinion of the owner, the owner could take charge of the work after three days notice, could employ labor as necessary and had the right to the materials and the detailed drawings by [Coughlin and] Ayres."[79][80] Further corroboration of the terms of this contract were documented in the Coughlin & Ayres's ledger, 1899-1901. At the top of Ayres' ledger entry was inscribed "J. M. Nix." The firm's accounting books record two residences were to be built by the contractor W. B. Massey, beginning December 30, 1899, and were to be finished by March 15, 1900, at the cost of $4,700.00.[81] The plumbing contractor, R. Strohmeyer, was to be paid $455.00, the electrical work was to be done by Shafer and Braden for $55.00, and on March 21, 1900, mantels and grates were to be provided by John H. Erb for $300.00.[82] This finding confirms that not only was Ayres involved in the construction but was directly administering the disbursement of funds to the contractors. The contract to build the houses rested with the architect's ability to get the job done and control the contractors.

In contrast, this is not the typical structure of most building agreements today. If Ayres were alive in this first decade of the twenty-first century and he was presented with a similar commission, the contracts would be written quite differently. First, today's owner-contractor agreements for this type of private construction project are private instruments and not recorded as a public record. Second, using today's conventions, the owner generally would have a separate contract with the general contractor and the contractor would take the leading role during construction. Third, and perhaps most significant, the owner today would place a significant amount of liability on the contractor for performance at the construction site whereas the architect would play a monitoring and certifying function (essentially, the architect would have administrative duties not directly involved in the act of building itself).[83] When J. M. and Birdie retained Ayres in 1899, the structure of the agreement represented a condition where the

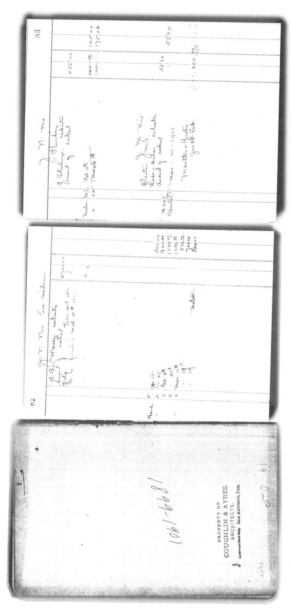

14. *Coughlin & Ayres Ledger, 1899. (Institute of Texan Cultures)*

architect played a more direct role in building—a condition seen only in today's design-build contracts where allocation of risk and liability are concentrated in one entity.[84]

A century after the Nix Houses, the architectural profession has sufficiently distanced itself from the business of construction so that the typical owner can no longer rely on an architect's leadership in the construction field. Time and again, we see owners engage "construction managers" instead of architects because they feel the need to have adequate protection against such lack of construction expertise. This is not true for all architectural firms, but it is certainly how the vast majority of design entities are treated by the owner and contractor; today, most general or sub-consulting contractors would dismiss the notion of being "controlled" by the architect during the construction phase.[85]

To be sure, the rapid-fire construction of the two Nix dwellings of mansion-like character within the first quarter of 1900 appears daunting even by today's standards. The discussion that follows reveals the necessity for construction techniques of 1899 to combine efficiency in erection for a timely delivery, yet hold to time-honored craftsmanship. The two concepts were continually at odds with one another as the twentieth century unfolded in the aftermath of the late Victorian struggle to reconcile craft and art with commerce and industry. Today we see the same professional debate utilizing handmade or unique construction components versus manufactured building elements.

V. ARCHITECTURAL IMPORTANCE OF THE NIX HOUSES

The Nix Houses—indeed every dwelling that can tell a story—are important for numerous reasons. First, this 1899 development deal is important to examine as it embodies a society in a state of radical change. It is a snapshot of shifting social values. From the lofty theoretical notions to the mundane and practical ideas of development, these homes offer more than shelter.

Second, the Nix Houses capture a pivotal moment in the history of American design and construction of single-family dwellings for the upper middle classes that were built at the end of the Victorian era.[86] The Nix Houses are significant because they incorporate mass-produced building elements that were intended to be perceived as handmade and to extol the virtues of customization. They capture an era of late nineteenth-century building arts unmatched in quality, style, and economy for upper middle income dwellings. This era brought dramatic changes to the production of building materials best illustrated by factory produced elements that offered a broad appeal without the expense of customization.[87]

Third, in no other period is there greater convergence of mass-made building material fabricated to appear handmade than in the late nineteenth century and early twentieth—a highly innovative period in the building trades stretching from 1870 to 1920 where pattern books and catalogues of domestic elements refinery were reaching the emerging middle and high income classes.[88] The subsequent demand for suitable houses, the growth of the first suburbs ,and the virtual doubling of the population resulted in a massive building boom during this time.[89]

Fourth, another important aspect of the Nix Houses, from a legal standpoint, is that their 1899 construction cannot be repeated. The existing historic structures were built nearly to the full width of the lots creating a bifurcated site plan with only a narrow slot between the two houses—a distance no greater than to service horse-drawn carriages. Such a narrow configuration was allowable in 1899 because there were no zoning laws that prescribed the calculation for front, side, or rear yard setbacks. The first zoning ordinance in the United States would come seventeen years later in 1916 with the adoption of the New York City Zoning Resolution. Many municipalities across the country modeled their local zoning ordinances based on New York City's soon after it came into force on the East Coast. Had the zoning ordinance in New York City been adopted two decades earlier, and depending on the degree of specificity with which the San Antonio municipality prescribed its setbacks, the Nix Houses could not have been built in their current form and location on the site.

Likewise, they are unrepeatable with current zoning regulations. After adoption of the Unified Development Code, or UDC, in San Antonio on May 3, 2001, and subsequent amendments and revisions (the latest occurring in 2005), the RM-4 zoning classification governs parcels upon which the Nix Houses stand.[30] Under the current zoning, the site could actually receive more built area. The bulk allowance under RM-4 zoned parcels must adhere to the following regulation: For every 4,000 square feet of site area, RM-4 allows a quadraplex, or 4 housing units per parcel. With the existing site area of each Nix House covering 7,100 square feet, (14,200 square feet inclusive of both parcels), it is feasible to increase the bulk of the built area at the site and create eight separate apartment units.

The current zoning regulations enacted by the City of San Antonio are intended to help stir redevelopment of inner-city neighborhoods by allowing more building area per parcel. The power to enact such regulatory legislation and mandate future owners to retroactively comport to newer zoning laws evokes the well known 1926 US Supreme Court case *Euclid v. Ambler,* affirming principles, statutes, and (zoning) ordinances to be elastic; the scope of their application must expand or contract to meet new and different conditions.[31] Logically, it follows that a neighborhood could be revitalized if it were more dense; having more tax-paying citizens clustered in smaller and denser areas downtown also has been shown to lower crime activity.

This idea has worked in other areas of the country, most notably New York City, where areas like East Harlem, under the initial guidance of Mayor Rudolf Guilianni, once rezoned have become the next hot neighborhood to live in thus attracting new residents, followed by new retail, then boutique restaurants, galleries, and shops.[92]

In 1899, placing four units on each site for a total of eight units would have been the equivalent of committing neighborhood heresy—perhaps it could have worked on another corner lot, but not on this smaller site on King William. For sure, the Steves family would not have fully accepted this scheme. As mentioned in the following chapter, their three homes were adjacent to the Nix houses. The Steves were much more financially and politically connected in the community than the newcomer Nixes and could have easily stopped the development. Building eight apartments on a luxurious, mansion-lined street would have been unheard of at the time. Despite this, J. M. and Birdie forged ahead with an innovative development idea, intending to take up residence amongst the renters, thus providing a direct solution to this problem.

Readers may be curious why the analysis that follows includes the smallest of details such as tile and wallpaper. Truth be told, for all real estate development, in all times, the devil has always remained in the details. Style, for better or worse, has taken the brunt and credit for the mistakes—and successes—that developers and architects have made in the past.

In terms of style, the Nix Houses are an excellent example of a fusion of custom works and mass-production. With Ayres embracing the innovations of the day, the dwellings are places where finely milled fireplaces of premium grade hardwoods can be mistaken for hand-carved mantels adorning a parlor room. This deception was not intentional but rather a function of the economy of construction and the need to meet a rising demand in housing stock owing to the economic expansion of the United States at the turn of the twentieth century coupled with the massive influx of the largest immigrant wave ever recorded in the U.S.[33] The new economy at the turn of the century created a newer, wealthier upper middle class. The mechanization of building components took over nearly every aspect of home decoration: Fancy parquet floor designs, decorative arts, stencils and wallpapers, ornamental over-mantels, and decorative heating devices took hold as the golden age of industrialization transformed every aspect of American life. To meet the need for new houses, Victorian-era speculative builders took advantage of the growing prosperity and made available to a growing number of wealthy families an abundance of styles and motifs that were easily transported. By the end of the Victorian era, simplicity of design had returned giving rise to the classical lines in vogue by 1900. The reaction against highly ornamental exteriors and eclectic styles of interior decoration made way for the birth of the modern movement and simpler lines at the beginning of the twentieth century.[34]

The Nix Houses represent some of the finest examples of the New England-style frame houses in South Texas. Planned in 1899, the

15. *New England Antecedent - A house in Ridgefield, Connecticut.*
434 and *432 King William are directly linked to the New England style frame house.*
Examples of this style, such as the 1880s house photographed above, reveal: (1) *promi-*
nent pediment facade; (2) *framed entry with double column motif and high pitched roof*
slope; and (3) *the use of paired windows and variegated wood siding shingles in select*
areas. These areas are design features Ayres imported from the Northeast. (*Roy*
Pachecano)

Nix Houses incorporated a strong symmetrical order on the main façades facing King William and adapted a wraparound veranda facing south for the hot climate. A typical New England home, such as the one referenced here, reveals striking similarities in form and design.

Furthermore, the design of the Nix Houses takes liberty in contrasting much of the Texas vernacular architecture and detailing. The design of the Nix Houses was endogenous and an uncommon style for South Texas. Design elements include the use of paired, unadorned columns, paired simplistic windows (without mid-section muntins), Palladian attic windows, bay window, massing of exterior, coloration of exterior, strong horizontal banding (wood siding, water table, cornices), regular and variegated shingles, and roof shape. These follow almost without exception, the high-pitched roofs of New England revival homes found during this same period.

The Nix Houses accommodated a non-native design for convenience. Examples of this include the roof shape (massing) and veranda (articulation). The scarcity of snow in South Texas makes the New England roof shape impractical, if not meaningless. In contrast, this climate with the abundance of sun dictated a less steep, lower profile roof design as seen in the flat roof, viga-style design that was more common during the preceding centuries; it had been modified continuously by the native Americans as well as the southern Mediterranean peoples that brought new ideas to this region.

The south-facing veranda, while not uncommon in New England revival homes to incorporate this feature, is really an adaptation of the

New England-style frame house to shield its most vulnerable façade from the significant, searing heat. The wraparound veranda helps to keep direct solar radiation from entering the main public space within the home—the front parlor.

The original fireplaces found at 432 and 434 are quintessential late Victorian, catalogue elements. The abundance of these decorative fireplaces at the Nix Houses (four original), represent an interior homage to an historic New England home where harsh winters forced the provision of heat in every room. In contrast to a severe cold season, the mild San Antonio winter offered relatively little need for domestic heat. To avoid breaking stylistic convention, provisions were made to suit the style of the home. Each fireplace is adorned on the exterior with decorative tiles in lieu of higher heat-tolerant stones or masonry. In 1899, the location of the fireplace in each room was of great importance to its enjoyment and was the most ornamental feature of the interior of the house; it was always given a prominent position, and carefully positioned so as not to be in the line of travel through the room, near the entrance door, or where a cross draft swept it.[95]

In general, the transition from solid fuel burning heat devices, which posed a fire hazard, to safer coal, followed by natural gas fuel sources triggered a stylistic change in fireplaces in the late nineteenth century in the United States. The shift from wood-burning fuel which necessitated a deeper and more substantial firebox, fireplace floor, and hearth to coal, namely anthracite, which could accommodate a much narrower firebox assembly, heralded the use of more refined materials to adorn the fireplace. Summer covers for grates became elaborate and distinguishable by the use of pressed steel with seasonal or allegorical themes.[96]

Since anthracite produced a steady, less volatile heat signature, delicate glazed tile began to find its way on fireplace hearths and surrounds in lieu of the heavier masonry and stone used centuries before. The shift in fuel had, by the late nineteenth century, become the principal fuel used in home heating and had, itself, become an industry that built many great fortunes.[97]

The need to harness this fuel prompted a design solution. Anthracite is a hard, compact variety of mineral coal that has a high glossy luster. It has the highest carbon count, contains the fewest impurities, and ignites with difficulty, burning with a short, blue, and smokeless flame. This type of coal differs from wood in that it needs a draft from the bottom. A grate design was invented to accommodate hard coal to insure an even and proper temperature that would expel pure air with the greatest economy of fuel.[98]

The Nix Houses' fireplace styles reflect this shift in domestic heat by incorporating decorative tile surrounds manufactured by the American Encaustic Tiling Company (A. E. Tile Co.). In 1880, A. E. Tile Co. began producing glazed or enameled tile specifically for use in such decorative locations within the home.[99] The first tiles of this type made by A. E. Tile Co. were used for flooring.[100] Since the hearth (the horizontal floor element immediately outside the firebox) of the fireplace often did not come from a catalogue, decorative tiles were used for both hearth and surrounds. A. E. Tile Co.[101] [102] produced four grades of tile: (1) Unglazed, such as is used for floors; (2) Glazed, which is what you see on earthenware; (3) Enamel, which is best, being of the same white potter's clay as fine china with a surface of transparent enamel in the soft tints of old gold, blue, pink, French gray, umber, olive, rich brown, and many others; and (4) Majolica, a raised enameled surface and differing from the enamel in having various figures and patterns in relief on its surface and in being more expensive. The fireplace surrounds at the Nix Houses are of the enamel type A. E. tile.—a remarkable finding in an 1899 South Texas home.

The fireplace mantels follow the design of the standard width of a chimney at the time—five feet. The original fireplaces were designed for coal-burning heat and were sized accordingly with the openings for coal grates, being twenty-six inches wide, thirty inches high, and twelve inches deep—i.e., the field measurements of fireplaces at the Nix Houses corroborate findings of late nineteenth-century factory-milled mantels found in trade catalogues of the time.[103] [104] Architects freely consulted trade catalogues to efficiently specify these ornate fireplaces which were assembled at the millshop[105] where they were built to tolerances to 1/16" and 3/32". The pre-assembly allowed the location of each brass screw to be predetermined.[106]

An analysis of the wallpaper revealed the Nixes had simplified taste, neither extreme nor subtle. The remnants of late nineteenth-century wallpaper were extracted from the construction site in 2006. A glimpse into the decorative arts at the time tells us that, like the A. E.

tile, fireplaces, and ornamental millwork, the wallpaper was fabricated in such a way that the printing process created minute variations with each roll. The fabrication process at the time was accomplished using a roller print that had felt on the inside and brass edging. The paper, usually a wood pulp variety (consistent with the sample from the site), would be printed in layers. The ink, a gouache-like pigment, would be pressed onto the wood pulp paper and leave behind an impression along with raised ink at the edges of the pattern.[107] The decorative paper was deemed neither wildly expensive nor dirt cheap but middle-of-the-road. The result is that the Nixes spent more on the fireplaces, millwork, and tile than on the decorative wall finish—which seems more than appropriate for a property conceived as a rental.

VI. OWNERS AND OCCUPANTS
OF 432 AND 434 KING WILLIAM

The construction of the houses at 432 and 434 King William were the first known ground-up construction projects by the Nixes on land which had been purchased and services procured for the purposes of speculative development. The twin houses were constructed primarily as rental properties although J. M. and Birdie lived at 432 from the time of completion in 1900 until 1907. The concept of developing a pair of rental homes in an area predominantly composed of mansions was bold and innovative. This strategy went against the owner-occupied mansion building type in the area. Erecting income-producing dwellings in a local market that was composed of luxury housing stock was simply contrary to the conventional wisdom in 1899; it was tantamount to committing neighborhood heresy—the equivalent of building a freeway over a cemetery and releasing the demons amongst us. Under similar guise, we would liken this today to the tear down phenomenon occurring in older communities to build "McMansions."[108]

While there is no evidence of resentment that this development project was built so close to the other single family dwellings, there is sufficient evidence to support the speculation that the neighbors were not exactly thrilled with the concept. The surrounding villas were built and owned by the proud and distinguished Steves family (pronounced *Sch-tee-ves*)—the patriarchal German family who controlled much of the lumber market in San Antonio during the late nineteenth century and which still mills doors and sashes today. There is little doubt the German-American family was eyeing the last vacant corner of King William. The senior Steves wanted to acquire two of the three lots opposite their homestead on King William and East Johnson for the purpose of giving these parcels, with a new house on each, as wedding presents to Edward, Jr., and Albert. The third son, Ernest, did not marry and continued to live in the family home with his parents. The clear observation on this street corner was that if Ernest Steves had married as well, Edward and Joanna Steves would have acquired all three vacant corner lots for their married children; hence, the parcels upon which the Nix Houses stand would not have been available for J. M. and Birdie Nix to develop. The Steves family did not stop the development. Nor could they. To make it more interesting, J. M. and Birdie Nix decided to take up residence in their own development deal which would have sufficiently suppressed any of the opposition since they had become King William residents in their own right. In 1903, J. M. and Birdie filed paperwork naming 432 King William as their "homestead."[109]

The ownership of the properties changed hands through the years. The house at 432 King William went from Nix to Gleason in 1907, from Gleason to Hill in 1918, from Hill to Hardy in 1921, and from Hardy to Bouquet in 1943, the last named living in the home until 2006.[110] The house at 434 King William went from Nix to Flores in 1912, from Flores to Gutierrez to Lozano to Garcia all in 1946, and from Garcia to Carvajal in 1948.[111]

With the purchase of 432 King William in 1943 by the Bouquet family and the purchase of 434 King William in 1948 by the Carvajal family, the ownership of the homes stabilized and became primary family residences.

Mrs. Carvajal and other members of her family made 434 King William their home until it was sold on August 15, 2005, to Portico Residential LLC, the current owner. Portico Residential is in the midst of restoring the 434 King William edifice to its former grandeur and similarly plans to restore 432 King William.[112] The Carvajal family was in residence at 434 King William for nearly 60 years—and most definitively holds the record for longest tenured homeowner. Interviews with Alfonso Carvajal, the brother of the late Mary Christine Carvajal, indicate the family's lineage linked to the Canary Islanders who arrived in this area in 1731.[113] [114]

16. *Photograph, 434 King William. Year of photo taken believed to be late 1940s; Studebaker introduced new styling for the 1947 model, highlighted by the wraparound rear-windowed Starlight coupe shown. (From the Estate of Mary Christine Carvajal, Patricia Carvajal Tindall, Trustee)*

VII. THE RESTORATION EFFORT

The primary motive in redeveloping the Nix Houses was to resurrect the dwellings as the first certified green, luxury, 1890s historic residences in the State of Texas. Since older buildings, like the Nix Houses, are notorious for not being energy conscious, having been erected at a time when energy commodities were relatively inexpensive, the primary motivation came from a compelling question: Can a drafty old home become state-of-the-art and incorporate today's energy efficient materials and designs without losing its intrinsic historic character? In short, can you remake a classic?

Portico Residential LLC took up the challenge of restoring these historic dwellings and was intent on going beyond the normal green approach taken by other builders whose method of green deployment is overwhelmingly in new, ground-up construction unfettered with the overlapping complexities of dealing with existing, historic buildings. Municipalities in fact have jumped on the bandwagon of developing green low-income affordable housing—all of which makes good sense. (More on specific green strategies later in this chapter.) Since its acquisition, Portico Residential has embarked on an exterior restoration program aimed at repositioning the house to its former clean, crisp state while upgrading all the critical building components such as mechanical, electrical, plumbing, structural, and accessory infrastructure systems. The integration of 21st century building technology will help to achieve new meaning and significance for these buildings so that they will survive well past 2100.

Beginning in 2005, plans were drafted to fully restore the properties as legal, single-family dwellings. In short order, the first item of business became reverting the SROs (Single Room Occupancy) back to single-family dwellings. Approval was granted on September 7, 2005, by the City of San Antonio's Historic and Design Review Commission (HDRC) to demolish the rear, 1950s, SRO addition attached to the main house of 434 King William. Next came the analysis of the site: its limitations, solar orientation, and the larger contextual picture which extended into the surrounding streetscape—the public domain and the removal of utility poles.

For much of the twentieth century, the utilities were granted unswaying and unprecedented access to the public domain. Of course, the historic homes were on King William before the utility poles and aerial cables were built. The first utility to arrive on King William was natural gas lines which ran down, and within, the unpaved streets. These "mains" had branch lines for each home that had an ability to burn gas. The sensibility of burying all subsequent utilities stopped there as miles upon miles of electrical cables and telecommunications lines have been strewn upon the historic streetscape. Sometime in the early 1920s, new electrical lines were hung to electrify private homes.

(Gas street lamps were still in use at that time but slowly waning in favor of the newer, safer electrical street lamps.)

What stemmed from the site analysis grew a challenging proposition of the restoration program: removal and burial of all overhead utilities at this significant corner site. This civic gesture would tie into the historic restoration of the property while adding to its cutting-edge technology by laying in empty conduit for future fiber optics and bringing high bandwidth to the dwellings. The restored homes await the next pathways that will eventually replace copper wiring as the primary mode of the transfer of data.

The conversion project took 18 months to design, coordinate, and build. The result was a spectacular investment in the public domain which opened up view corridors and further enhanced the historic streetscape. The project entailed the removal of 14 utility poles, and burial of approximately 2,000 linear feet of aerial cable (one estimate places this figure at 10,000 linear feet owing to the cable redundancy found on many of the poles). The *San Antonio Express News* published an article highlighting before and after photographs that revealed the changed corner at East Johnson and King William[115]

The effort greatly linked, visually, the East Johnson corridor and the pedestrian bridge spanning the San Antonio River. The project has also served as a pilot program to study for a greater, King William-wide conversion which the local residents, together with the King William Association, are considering under a special committee. It is the author's hope that all utility poles and associated cables, transformers, low and high voltage lines, data and telecommunications wiring in the downtown San Antonio area will be buried with careful attention paid to enhancing the streetscape and precious pedestrian-friendly atmosphere that is unique to the city.

Some of the challenges facing the redevelopment project extended into the most fundamental building components. The structural system, for example, required comprehensive updating. In addition, the exterior and interior walls and ceilings required significant restoration. Added to these challenges was the overarching goal of going beyond green building standards ahead of the local municipality's adoption of green guidelines for historical structures.[116] National programs such as "LEEDS for Homes" (Leadership in Energy and Environmental Design for Homes) are being adopted by municipalities across the country but few, if any, have written and adopted specific codes for historic properties that date over a century old. The following pages offer a glimpse into the Nix Houses redevelopment and restoration strategy.

Green Building

The Nix Houses are incorporating green, sustainable building principles. Upon completion, they will be Texas's first certified green, 1890s historic houses that do not compromise the historic integrity of the dwellings. The dwellings will incorporate at least 18 green design principles for greater energy efficiency and less impact on the environment:

(1) Use of spray foam insulation to achieve high R-values (a unit of measure for insulation in all buildings; the higher the number, the greater the insulation value) at exterior walls—transfer technology from NASA which has been used in the design of the space shuttle fleet;

(2) Use of foam liners at all sole plates and stud wall joints (cripples, headers, sills) to eliminate air infiltration entering through walls at floors, windows, and doors;

(3) Design of insulated foundation walls and adjoining crawl spaces to minimize convected air heat gain/loss;

(4) Design of a non-vented roof attic;

(5) Design of energy efficient air-conditioning system;

(6) Installation of state-of-the-art home automation and monitoring;

(7) Incorporation of solar photovoltaics for direct current electricity;

(8) Highly reflective metal roof material above primary structure;

(9) Acrylic (non-petroleum based product) roofing material at open balconies and roof terraces;

(10) Tankless water heating system;

(11) Rainwater harvesting system;

(12) Site design to enhance prevailing winds for cross breezes;

(13) Thermal glass for greater reduction in heat gain at windows and doors;

(14) Preservation of existing 1899 windows with upgrades to decrease air infiltration;

(15) Use of tandem car garage which yields a more efficient, compact garage resulting in more garden space;

(16) Solar shading at exterior of historic, single-paned windows;

(17) Recycling of existing wood (from demolition of existing rear sheds) for framing new construction which minimizes construction debris;

(18) Restoration, not replacement, of 95% of the 1890s historic home interior and exterior.

Structure

All original cedar posts have been replaced with concrete piers. This work was triggered by years of wood rot (brought on by exposure to water in the ground), significant termite damage, and building settlement. The original structure utilized a balloon framing technique (described below) with raw material culled from the local Beitel lumberyard.[17] It is interesting to note that these rough-hewn members have such density and structural capacity that they perhaps are equivalent to the combined strength of structural members twice their size. Further, if one were to plane a sample of these rough-framing units, there would appear a fine grain that is even, remarkably parallel, and wholly without knots. It is well known in the lumber business that this age, type, and species of wood can no longer be found and that the wood used for rough framing during this time would likely exceed in quality the stock available for today's finished millwork. After remarkably being in place for over a century, the original framing members have retained their original dimensions, shape, and strength.

Today, it is difficult to find a straight 25-30 foot stud, much less the hundreds required to be milled for use in construction. At the Nix Houses, yellow long-leaf pine was the primary structural material and the lengths found in this lumber, without knots and with true parallel grain composition, meant that it could have only been harvested from trees that were least 125 years old. It is highly probable that at the time of construction, the lumber being installed at the Nix Houses were sapling trees during the time the Continental Congress met in

Philadelphia to ratify the United States Constitution which began to function in 1789.

The balloon framing technique is a system of wood construction, predominately utilized in the 19th century, where studs are continuous from the foundation sill to the top wall plate creating an exterior exo-skeleton. Numerous floor levels would be hung from the studs and set up a condition where the exterior walls would commonly be support-ed by 25-30 foot wood members in two-story structures with attic space.

The balloon framed technique replaced the time-honored post-and-beam technique and was made possible by the availability of structural lumber sawed to uniform sizes. Today, we see harvested and recycled wood members that are limited in length because of environ-mental laws which prohibit the harvesting of older, more mature hard-wood forests. A balloon frame, which is held together entirely by nails and cuts made on a module of 2 inches, could be erected faster with the use of less-skilled labor. In contrast, the preferred framing tech-nique of choice prior to balloon framing was the post-and-beam frame which relied on mortise and tenon construction detailing where the use of nails was limited and structural integrity was achieved with intricate, time-consuming joinery. The end result with the balloon technique was a stronger structural system than the mortise and tenon type and more apt to be square and plumb. However efficient its erec-tion which made it a popular system, the balloon technique has one serious drawback: Unless firestops are installed at the level of every floor, the stud spaces that are formed between the members are essentially chimneys from the cellar to the attic, greatly accelerating the spread of potential fire.

At the Nix Houses, this old framing technique has been modified to adapt to current codes and much care has been taken to weave a new, modified platform framing system into the existing shell. Thus, restoring the historic structural system proved to be a challenge: the conversion of a balloon frame to a platform frame and effectively doubling the structural capacity.

Exterior

Approximately 95% of the buildings' exterior has been restored (not replaced). This arduous task has led to the stripping of nearly 10 coats of paint and the gentle re-sanding of the exterior long-leaf cedar and yellow pine siding covering a vertical surface area in excess of 15,000 square feet. Where wood siding was destroyed, it has been replaced with the same century-old plank and identical shape found on the site. No artificial materials have been used in the restoration of the exterior; exterior siding of the house is original, long-leaf cedar and has been painstakingly restored. The houses have not been moved; they rest in their original location. The exterior appearance retains the essential physical features of its original design and materials.

Interior

Approximately 75% of the original interior was restored to its 1899 design. Where we deviated from Ayres' original plans was to accommodate 21st century technology:

(1) A "hub wall" was outfitted to house a home automation system which ties electrical, lighting, HVAC, security, audio and home entertainment together. This state-of-the-art system can monitor all the building's systems from around the world;

(2) Reclamation of an unused attic with a lot of storage potential;

(3) All 1899 fireplaces restored to their original state (with some coal grates missing). The fire boxes have been electrified. Chimney flues have been adapted for vertical chases to run HDMI and category 6 twisted copper for data transmission. Overmantels have built-in flat panel televisions which are, in turn, wired to the home automation system so that the interface allows the occupant to download a movie without the need to insert a DVD into any player (the author believes DVDs, like copper wiring, are already outdated);

(4) Allowances were made within the existing layout of the walls and ceilings to run empty conduits for future fiber optic structured cabling;

(5) The interior staircase, millwork, and window surrounds have all been preserved. With few exceptions, all of the interior window casements were restored including counterweights and pulley systems;

(6) Interior wood sheathing remains intact in 90% of the dwellings. This 1" x 6" yellow pine sheathing helped provide structural support in the balloon frame;

(7) All doors, door hardware, and transoms have been carefully restored. Where we made new openings in original walls, we matched period inserts for opening jambs, headers, and thresholds;

(8) All bathrooms are new as nothing was salvageable;

(9) All kitchens are brand new and include Subzero refrigerator and beverage coolers, as well as professional cooking ranges;

(10) No expense was spared at upgrading the finishes. All the stone in the houses is marble or limestone—there is no granite in the houses. Portico Residential consulted with its Polish stone fabricator in New

York who brought in from Italy the finest, durable, most elegant slabs of Calacutta Borghini, Verdi Classico, and a blue-hued limestone; and finally

(11) Four original chandeliers that hung in the Plaza Hotel in New York City were acquired through Christie's auction house and are installed at the Nix Houses to lace the restoration with a sense of authenticity and enduring elegance.

Mechanical, Electrical, Plumbing (MEP)

All MEP systems were carefully installed with sensitivity given to historic components of the home. None of the ceilings are furred-out to cover an easy duct-run—there was nothing easy about installing the SEER 19 Trane three-zoned units. All the duct work is carefully woven into the existing historic structure so that none of the original Ayres's detailing was lost; no furr-downs in ceilings or furring of walls was created to "hide" ductwork. The tremendous R-values achieved by installing the unique foam insulation afforded the design of the HVAC components to become very efficient.

New Rear Addition

To take advantage of lot area and newer allowable density, a new rear addition is being built to National Historic Preservation Guidelines. On September 7, 2005, approval was granted by the City of San Antonio's Historic Design and Review Commission to build a new rear addition to the Ayres' main house. The new addition features a private terrace with an open-air wood-burning fireplace. It will have a private balcony overlooking East Johnson and a glimpse of the foot-bridge crossing San Antonio's famous Riverwalk. The new rear addition has the capacity to function as a studio or live-in quarters for an elderly family member. In this way, the restoration project reflects a growing trend back toward multi-generational family living.

Solar Energy

With energy costs rising, it made sense to infuse the green design with solar energy. The view held by the author concerning the decision to incorporate this useful technology was on one hand philosophical and on the other practical. "Going solar" is analogous to the late nineteenth-century shift in energy sourcing from wood to coal mentioned in the previous chapter. When coal was replaced with electricity in the twentieth century this represented another shift brought on by a greater efficiency in fuel source. In the first decade of the twenty-first century, it seems natural to shift again to more efficient fuel sources. Incorporating solar photovoltaic panels, or PV cells, in an historic restoration program also appears at odds with the goal of most preservationists. Finding an appropriate solution to inherent design conflicts such as where to place PV panels on an historic roof can be resolved. The restoration program of the Nix Houses includes PV cells because the energy return on investment will pay for itself while simultaneously helping to reduce environmental emissions that may be leading to global warming. By incorporating these green building features, the restoration project will be the first historic home built with the charm of the nineteenth century and wholly embracing the technology of the twenty-first century.

Landmark Status

The research, planning, and subsequent instauration culminated in receiving Landmark Status. At the end of 2006, the Texas Historical Commission designated the property an official state historical landmark. As this book goes to press, planning is underway for a ceremonial unveiling of a cast medallion. This special status, awarded to properties deemed worthy of preservation for their architectural integrity and historical importance, conveys a measure of legal protection to the property. The designation is also intended to protect the cultural legacy of the place. At this writing, Texas Historical Commission (THC) only recognizes 434KW, but plans are afoot to seek the designation for 432KW as well.

Despite the lack of THC designation for 432KW, it is still protected by virtue of its presence, in situ, within the boundaries of the King William Historic District. Remarkably, many professionals and lay persons alike have a misunderstanding of how historic districts really work, legally. The first legislation that created "landmark districts" was adopted by New York City in 1965 when then-Mayor Robert Wagner signed into local law the creation of the Landmarks Preservation Commission. The original intent of the local ordinance —which has the same effect as law—seeks to protect a collective group of parcels that are deemed to have intrinsic value as a cultural asset regardless of style and, to a great extent, regardless of age. In New York, as became true in many other parts of the country including San Antonio, these laws were enacted in response to a growing concern that important physical elements of the city's history were being lost despite the fact that these buildings could be reused. Such historic districts—having all been created locally—come into existence not entirely because of the aesthetic merits they possess but because of the underlying cultural heritage attached to them. Dwellings and other structures caught within the metes and bounds of a historic district are parcels automatically protected by the legislative enactment of their particular municipality. This goes for virtually any structure be it Victorian, Colonial, or 1950s modern. Thus, in a hypothetical situation: A small 1960s bungalow that does not have an individual designation also carries protection in the same manner as its adjoining neighbor, a hypothetical Victorian mansion built a century earlier that may have a medallion affixed to its facade; if they are within the same historic district, regardless of a state or federal individual designation, they are both legally protected.

The degree of protection varies with each parcel. Individual landmarks often have more strict guidelines regarding alterations and most, if not all, municipalities clearly distinguish between individual landmark buildings, such as the Empire State Building or the Alamo, and historic districts. Each municipality also promulgates its own criteria for evaluating a building and the rules they apply. These rules have been tested over time through case law.[118]

 The contribution to Texas history at the Nix Houses tells a story of how two alien structures came to embody a transitional cultural moment in the late nineteenth century, at the zenith of industrialized America, where manufactured products were replacing the handmade world. How to make an outdated nineteenth-century relic relevant in the twenty-first century has become woven into the story: The restoration offers a new way to resolve an old tension between traditional (handmade) objects and mass-produced (manufactured) building products. The last chapter of this story tells of the embracing of modern technology allowing the dwellings to be highly energy efficient and environmentally sound. The houses have been restored in a spirit that transforms the dwellings without the excessive taking of our natural resources and, in this way, the houses themselves offer something back to our world.

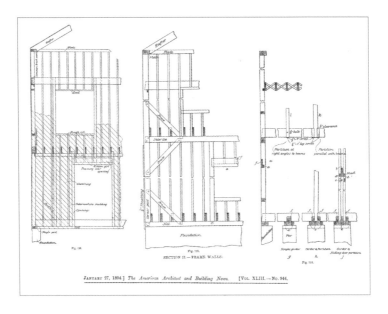

17. *Atlee B. Ayres was very familiar with contemporary trade publications and would have studied current issues in Avery Library at Columbia University. Drawings above illustrate the typical two-story balloon frame technique which was used to build the Nix Houses. Published January 27, 1894, in the American Architect and Builder. (Avery Architectural Fine Arts Library, Columbia University, New York)*

18. *Computer animation (still), 432 King William, proposed interior courtyard. (Portico Residential LLC)*

19. *Computer animation (still), 432 King William, proposed trellised turn-around driveway/courtyard. (Portico Residential LLC)*

20. *Page 134 of Christie's catalogue commemorating The Plaza Hotel's auction that took place on March 15, 2006, in New York. The historic auction sold off fixtures from the landmark hotel such as door knobs, mirrors, and paintings. Here, lot 272 showing chandeliers that hung in the lobby corridor (with an inset image of the Beatles in front of the chandeliers) acquired by Portico Residential to lace the restoration work of the Nix Houses. (Christie's, New York)*

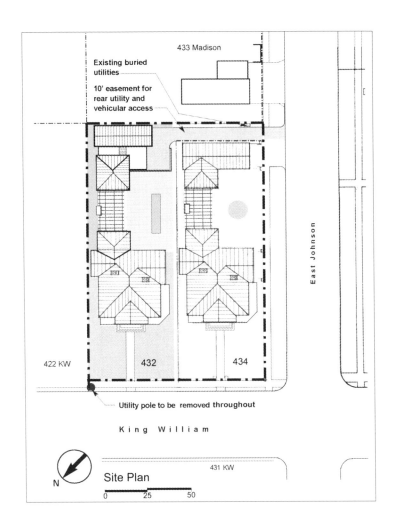

21. *Drawing, Site Plan, 432 and 434 King William.*
(Roy Pachecano)

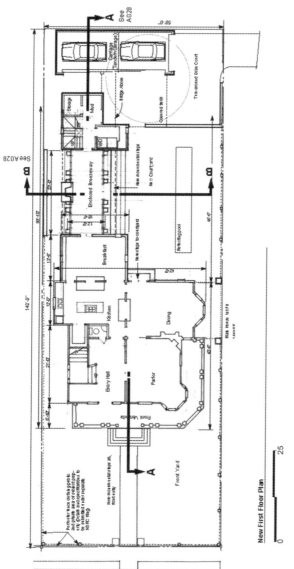

22. *Drawing, First Floor plan, 432 King William. (Roy Pachecano)*

23. *Drawing, Front elevation, 434 King William. (Roy Pachecano)*

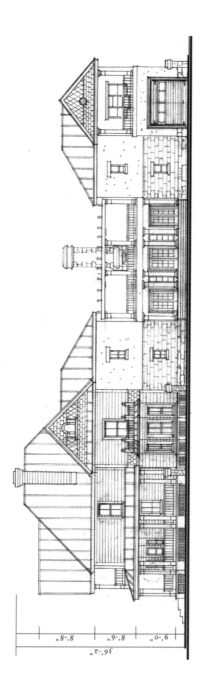

24. *Drawing, Elevation (Side view), 434 King William. (Roy Pachecano)*

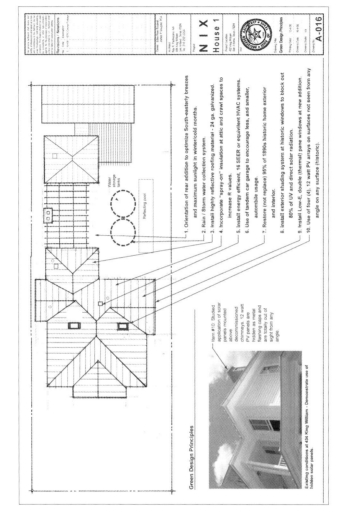

Green Design Principles

1. Orientation of rear addition to optimize South-easterly breezes and maximum sunlight in winter/cold months.

2. Rain / Storm water collection system.

3. Install highly reflective roofing material - 24 ga. galvanized.

4. Incorporate "spray-on" insulation at attic and crawl spaces to increase R values.

5. Install energy efficient, 16 SEER or equivilent HVAC systems.

6. Use of tandem car garage to encourage less, and smaller, automobile usage.

7. Restore (not replace) 95% of 1890s historic home exterior and interior.

8. Install exterior shading system at historic windows to block out 80% of UV and direct solar radiation.

9. Install Low-E, double (thermal) pane windows at new addition.

10. Use of four (4), 12 watt PV arrays on surfaces not seen from any angle on any surface (historic).

Item #10. Studied application of solar panels mounted above decommissioned chimneys. 12 watt PV panels are hidden as metal flashing caps and are totally out of sight from any angle.

Existing conditions at 434 King William - Demonstrate use of hidden solar panels.

25. Drawing, Green design principles, the Nix Houses. (Roy Pachecano)

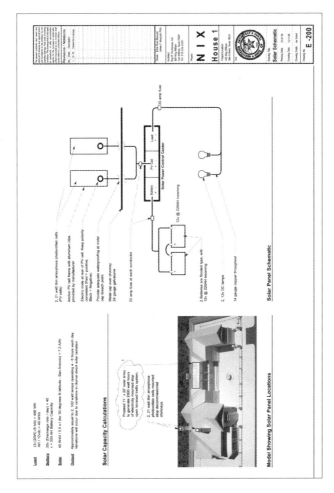

26. Drawing, Solar design, the Nix Houses. (Roy Pachecano)

27. Photograph, "Before" architectural columns. 434 King William. (Roy Pachecano)

28. *Photograph, "After" architectural columns, 434 King William. (Roy Pachecano)*

29. Photograph, "Before" building envelope, 434 King William. (Roy Pachecano)

30. *Photograph, "After" building envelope, 434 King William. (Roy Pachecano)*

VIII. AFTERWORD

Perhaps at no other time in the history of building hand-crafted homes are the forces of mass-production harder at work to reverse the meaning of "custom home" than today. Looking back at the pivotal moment of the late 19th century when the Nix-Ayres team set out to build, the term of "art" for anything custom was much better understood. Perhaps our values have changed. In today's parlance, the use of the term "custom home" has disfigured the intent of the original meaning so much that anything custom today often resembles something else. This distorts the original meaning of the words which were intended to convey uniqueness and originality. A drive down any suburban enclave or gated community suggests uniformity, monotony, and severity that triggers the following question: How did we lose the love of craft and the art of making a dwelling infused with meaning?

The departure to the suburbs in the mass-exodus from the inner-city at the middle half of the 20th century cannot be the sole culprit. The migration, under various terms such as "white flight" or "urban diaspora", is historically linked to market conditions to which developers are attuned. Developers too cannot be singled out as the sole party responsible for this demise of quality over quantity—although, arguably, they have contributed much in the way of limiting the number of choices the consumer is offered. The physical manifestation of the decay of the inner city is a result of its equal and opposite powerful destructive force: suburban sprawl. The demands a society places on what it values most certainly have changed. The populist shift from an agrarian society to an industrial one has been viewed by many social historians as one of the most influential circumstances in modern life—and we are still reeling under the effects. The technological optimism of the nineteenth century may be likened to the market enthusiasm of the twenty-first century. The markets today, like the railroads of yesteryear, make useful tools, but discipline is needed to use their power to fit into a larger environmental policy.[119] To understand our land use is to know who we are and to be able to fit this into the larger picture of our American history.[120]

We are limited to the amount of sprawl we can sustain. Restoring our inner city appears to be one of the most sustainable efforts we can undertake if cities are to have a future. It takes restoring one building at a time. People are crying out for authenticity. So much out there is phony. The preponderance of the suburban nation and the rise of sprawl have eviscerated our cities, neighborhoods, and blocks—right down to our homes. Yet, there is this yearning for things that are real, substantive. How else could a culture, embroiled in a vision of reality television, become transfixed, motionless, in its daily commute to and from work? Our modern reliance on vast corridors of expressway, where the occupant is transient, has belied our innate desire for permanence at our arrival point: the home. Yet the automobile isn't the prime culprit either.

Homes, apartment dwellings, and their general construction today are far from being built as permanent edifices. Few will substantively last the five-year adjustable-rate mortgage that financed its purchase. Fewer still will perform beyond the 30-year fixed note that is the cornerstone of real estate home finance. As "homebuilders" strive to roll out production homes, they employ gimmicks such as a refrigerator camouflaged as an armoire to fill the spiritual void left by the home itself.[121] The homebuilder will do whatever it takes to sell the production home in order to reconcile the high cost of infrastructure, and keep pace of the "churn"—tactics intended to distract potential buyers away from the poor architecture and frail construction preponderant in today's production house.

It was suggested in the mid-1980s that the long process of suburbanization would slow down. Rising energy costs in the wake of the first oil embargo by OPEC during the 1970s coupled with higher land costs would lead people back to urban centers.[122] As the pattern has emerged over the past 20 years, Americans have moved, increasingly, to the distant fringes of metropolitan regions more than ever before while, simultaneously, the older, often historic, downtowns have lost population, jobs, and vital economies.[123]

It is interesting to observe that in no other country on the planet is the inner city precinct so often linked to the ghetto or enclave for the lower classes. Because this story involves property in an affluent enclave in the center of one of America's oldest cities, it may serve as an interesting counterpoint to most housing developments in the United States. Similarly, the inner city in most, if not all, major European centers is where the affluent live. In contrast, most of the affluent live outside city-center in the United States. So, it was with disbelief, as told by the 2005 global news event coming out of France, that most Americans saw the Paris suburbs breaking out in riots. Most watching CNN did not stop to think that the suburbs in Europe were where the working class live. Why we have an inverse urban planning condition is not the focus of this book but it underscores the value of location.

Location has an impact on livability, community, and connectivity. Cities have nerve centers analogous to organs of the human body. Take out a heart, the specimen dies. Uncontrolled growth likely leads to obesity. A brain-dead town cannot be kept alive by artificial life forever. The challenge then becomes how to develop sustainable communities. I believe it all starts within the home itself; somewhere between the entry door and sleeping area, there is a gathering place that genuinely feels like home. This too the Nixes and Ayres gave us: that homes need not be artificial—they can form a real place.

The Nix Houses serve as an example of living within our environment, restoring our heritage, building green, offering authenticity, conserving resources, and being connected by history and location.

IX. APPENDIX

Endnotes

Acknowledgements

1. Omar Pachecano's father, the late J. Natividad Pachecano, a native of San Luis Potosí, Mexico, born December 25, 1896, was trained as a mason like his father before him, Luciano Pachecano. In 1950 he established N. Pachecano, Concrete Contractor. In 1954, he formed N. Pachecano & Sons, Concrete Contractors, and worked alongside his sons: Luciano (held a temporary position), Ruben, Nat, Homer, and Omar. In 1958 the entity became N. Pachecano & Sons, Inc., and continued the family tradition of construction well into the late twentieth century. The author's great-grandfather, Luciano Pachecano, and great-great-grandfather before him, Paoblo Pachecano, were also skilled masons having carved stone in the old-world manner as immigrants to Mexico. The Pachecano surname, having its origins in Naples, Italy (Pacchiano), has traveled through Spain and Mexico before arriving in the United States in 1910. Pachecanos have been associated with construction for over six generations extending back almost 200 years. Omar, the tenth of twelve children was born on Sweet Street on November 25, 1934, only a few blocks away from the subject matter of this book. Omar Pachecano continues the family tradition under Portico Residential LLC.

2. The article in the *SanAntonio Express News,* October 18, 2006, "Private Project Enhances Street," by Michelle Mondo, illustrates the need for public-private partnerships to exist if older, historic communities are to succeed in bringing about utility overhead conversion and thus restore the vital streetscape.

I. Context and City

3. See *King William Historic District* by Christopher Long in the Handbook of Texas Online. The district was originally part of the *labor de abajo,* or lower labor (farmlands) assigned to the San Antonio de Valero Mission.

4. This intersection is a key turning point: On the self-guided maps published by the San Antonio Conservation Society, it is the only intersection where pedestrians cross paths on their circular journey through the King

William Historic District. It is also the beginning point of what was dubbed "Sauerkraut Bend" in the late nineteenth and early twentieth centuries owing to the predominant German homeowners residing along the San Antonio River where it makes its last sweeping bend as it leaves the downtown precinct.

5. The Steves Homestead Museum is owned and operated by the San Antonio Conservation Society.

6. Lich, Glenn E. *The German Texans*, p.147.

7. The street name "Kaiser Wilhelm," was an affectionate term used by many of the affluent German residents for the street legally named King William. This naming was in honor of Kaiser Wilhelm I, one of Germany's important political figures in its modern history and Germany's penultimate King or Kaiser. Born in Berlin in 1797, Wilhelm I was proclaimed German Emperor in 1871 ten years after having ascended to the throne as King of Prussia. By this ceremony, the German territories were transformed into the German Empire. ("Kaiserreich", 1871-1918) [Wikipedia Encyclopedia, "Wilhelm I of Germany"] There was a great swelling of pride and nationalism amongst people descending from Germany and Prussia everywhere. Thus, the German community reflected this pride in the naming of this street.

8. King William Street was renamed Pershing Street in honor of General John J. Pershing during World War II when anti-German sentiment was strong. In 1921 the San Antonio City Council approved a name change to King William Street, the anglicized version of Kaiser Wilhelmstrasse. Green, *Place Names of San Antonio*, p. 10.

9. Koch, Augustus, "Bird's Eye View of San Antonio Bexar County, Texas 1886, Looking East."

10. Long, "King William Historic District." See Internet Resources below.

11. Burkholder, Mary V. and Graham B. Knight. *The King William Area*, p. 9.

12. Long, *King William Historic District*. See Internet Resources below.

13. Burkholder, Mary V., *Down the Acequia Madre in the King William Historic District*, p. 10.

14. Thomas J. Devine was an eminent Texas jurist and attorney who patented thousands of acres of land in Bexar, Frio, Uvalde, and Zavala counties in the mid- to late 1800s. Texas General Land Office, Austin, Tex. See biographical sketch by Yancey L. Russell in the Handbook of Texas Online.

15. Burkholder and Knight, *The King William Area*, p. 47.

16. Thomas J. Devine — "Deed with Vendor's Lien," — Charles & Adelia Cresson. 23 March 1878; Bexar County, Tex., Deed Book 7, p. 488. "Release of lien," 26 July 1879, Bexar County, Tex., Deed Book 14, p. 227, Bexar County Courthouse, San Antonio, Tex.

17. 1880 U.S. Census, Bexar County, Tex., p. 208A, Family History Library Film 1255291, National Archives Film T9-1291, accessed on the LDS Family Search website. Appearing in the 1880 household are: Charles C. Cresson, Adelia, wife, and children, son, Charles Cresson (age 7) and daughter Mary (age 4) along with Adelia's mother, Julia Van Derlip. Charles C. Cresson was a Major in the U.S. Army. Nearby families are predominately of Bavarian and Prussian ancestry. The Edward and Johanna Steves family lived ten households away, and like the Steves, the Cressons were active in both social and civic affairs in the community.

18. "C. C. and A. Cresson — V. L. Deed to Birdie L. Nix." 16 Sept. 1899, Bexar County, Tex., Deed Book 182, pp. 380-381, Bexar County Courthouse, San Antonio, Tex.

19. Telephone interview conducted in San Antonio, Tex., on 4/18/2006 by Roy Pachecano with Helen "Suzie" Brooks Piña of San Antonio. Mrs. Piña is the daughter of Josephine Nix Brooks and David Brooks, great-granddaughter of J. M. and Birdie Nix.

20. On Feb. 6, 1893, Birdie Nix purchased from J. L. Rose of Arapahoe County, Colorado, a parcel of land in San Antonio in the Paschal Lewis Addition on Dallas Street for $2,000. Bexar County Deed Book, Vol. 126, p. 85. No ground-up development is recorded at this time.

II. The Nix Family

21. Telephone interview conducted by Patricia Ezell with Christopher D. Ross of San Antonio on May 22, 2006. Christopher Ross is the son of Helen "Suzie" Brooks Piña, grandson of Josephine Nix Brooks and David Brooks, great-grandson of Joseph L. Nix and great-great-grandson of J. M. and Birdie Nix. J. M. Nix was the son of Joseph John Nix and Maggie Wisdom Nix. He was born in Childersburg, Talladega County, Alabama, in 1866 and died in Brownsville, Texas, on May 30, 1932. His full name was Joseph Madison Napoleon Bonaparte Nix. J. M. Nix married Birdie Lanier in 1890 in Huntsville, Madison County, Alabama. Birdie Williametta Lanier was the daughter of William H. Lanier and Marena Jane Saluter Ford. Birdie was born in October 1873 in Huntsville, Alabama, and died on August 8, 1952, in San Antonio. J. M. and Birdie Nix moved to Tennessee where he opened a shoe store. In the early 1890s J.M. and Birdie moved to San Antonio where he began using the initials "J.M." J. M Nix, Birdie Nix, and their only child, Joseph L. Nix, are buried in the Mission Park South cemetery on S.W. Military Highway, San Antonio, Tex.

22. Appler, Jules A., *General Directory and Blue Book, City of San Antonio*, 1903-1904.

23. Bailey, Ernest Emory, *Texas Historical and Biographical Record, With a Genealogical Study of Historical Family Records*, pp. 255-256.

24. Appler, Jules A. *General Directory of the City of San Antonio*, 1896.

25. 1900 U.S. Census, Bexar County, Tex., Roll 1612, p. 60, Line 18, Household 156, Family 156, microfilm images from the National Archives, Washington D.C. available through Heritage Quest Online.

26. 1910 U.S. Census, Bexar County, Tex., Roll 1532, p. 56, Line 62, Household 55, Family 64, microfilm images from the National Archives, Washington D.C. available through Heritage Quest Online.

27. Bailey, p. 255.

28. 1920 U.S. Census, Bexar County, Tex., Roll 1777, p. 196, Line 44, microfilm images from the National Archives, Washington D.C. available through Heritage Quest Online.

1930 U.S. Census, Bexar County, Tex., Roll 2295, p. 124, Line 21, microfilm images from the National Archives, Washington D.C. available through Heritage Quest Online.

29. Bailey, p. 255.

30. "More Hotels for San Antonio is Pressing Need – Business Men's Club Committee Discuss." *San Antonio Daily Express*, Saturday, March 2, 1907.

31. Bailey, pp. 255-256.

32. Telephone interview conducted in San Antonio, Tex., on 4/20/2006 by Roy Pachecano with Christopher D. Ross of San Antonio.

33. Norton, Chas. G., ed., *Men of Affairs of San Antonio.*

34. *San Antonio Express*, June 1, 1932, p. 3.

35. Odom, Marianne and Gaylon Finklea Young, "Medical Excellence Stands Tall at the Nix," *San Antonio Light*, Sunday, July 6, 1986.

36. Rust, Joe Carroll. *Historic Bexar County*, p. 87. The Smith-Young Tower was designed together with Atlee B. Ayres' son, Robert Ayres. It was, upon completion and until the mid-1950s, one of the tallest buildings west of the Mississippi River.

37. Fisher, Lewis F. *Riverwalk, The Epic Story of San Antonio's River*, pp. 25, 30, 86. Lewis Fisher's passionate account of San Antonio's "crown jewel" is a must-read for anyone interested in learning more about the history of the city's famed Riverwalk.

III. Financing the Deal

38. Rust, p. 41.

39. Brockman, John Martin. *Railroads, Radicals and Democrats: A Study in Texas Politics, 1865-1900*, p. iii.

40. Bailey, p. 255. The 1910 U.S. Census, Bexar County, Tex; Roll 1532, p. 56, Line 62, Household 55, Family 64, lists J. M. Nix's occupation as a "railroad promoter."

41. Allen, Paula, *San Antonio, Then and Now*, pp. 58-59, 90-91. The Sunset Depot is still in operation and is surrounded by offices and retail businesses in a renewed area of downtown. The old IG&N depot ceased operation in 1970. In the late 1980s, it was renovated and is the office of the San Antonio City Employees Credit Union.

42. Texas Transportation Museum, Longhorn Chapter, The M-K-T *(Missouri-Kansas-Texas)* Depot and History. Texas Transportation Museum website.

   Hemphill, Hugh. *The Railroads of San Antonio and South Central Texas*, pp. 55-65. The M-K-T depot was closed in 1964 and demolished in 1969. The only remaining remnants of the depot are a few railroad tracks on Arsenal Street behind the La Quinta Inn and Suites at 100 West Durango, a few tracks on Alamo Street farther south at Loop 410 and IH-35, and a beautiful doorway incorporated as a main window into one of the Boutique Galeria shops at Los Patios in San Antonio.

43. Buenger, Walter L., *The Path To A Modern South: Northeast Texas between Reconstruction and the Great Depression*, p. 46.

44. Livingston, James. *Pragmatism and The Political Economy of Cultural Revolution, 1850-1940*, p. 184.

45. Brueggeman and Fisher, *Real Estate Finance and Investments*, p. 497. The world of real estate finance and investments continues to evolve as capital and mortgages play an expanding role as investments in both private and public markets. Examples of this evolution can be seen in creation of capital market vehicles such as commercial mortgage-backed securities (CMBS) and real estate investment trusts (REITs) which did not exist in their current form merely twenty years ago.

46. Livingston, p. 185.

47. Board of Governors of the Federal Reserve System. "Banking and

Monetary Statistics, Money Rates and Security Markets, No. 120 – Short-term open-market rates in New York City, monthly, 1890-1941," Published by the Federal Reserve Archival System for Economic Research (FRASER), Annual Statistical Digest, P. 449. See Internet Resources below.

48. Historical information provided by the San Antonio Conservation Society, 418 Villita Street, San Antonio, Tex., 78205; telephone 210-224-5711. See Internet Resources below.

49. Fisher, p. 6.

50. Rust, p. 73.

51. Schmidt, F. A. "Rails to the Artesian Belt." Reference to oil discovery also available online at the Handbook of Texas Online. See Internet Resources below.

52. Rust, p. 79.

53. Texas State Data Center estimated the population of Bexar County to have exceeded 1.5 million in 2006. See Internet Resources below.

54. "The American Architect and Building News", January-March 1893, vol. XXXIX, no. 890, Ticknor & Co., Boston. Avery Architectural and Fine Arts Library, Columbia University.

55. Coote, Robert James, *The Eclectic Odyssey of Atlee B. Ayres, Architect*, p. 44. Ayres placed a high priority on a working library and keeping it current. He claimed to have the best architectural resource library in the State of Texas and was continually adding to it.

56. B. L. Nix to D. Hirsch, Bexar County Deed Record, Bk. 186, p. 478.

57. Once the property was transferred by W. B. Massey's assignment of lien to D. Hirsch, Hirsch had become owner of the note as well as beneficiary of the lien (W. F. Ezell, Notary Public, notarized document on April 18, 1901. Filed on April 22, 1901, by Frank McNewton, Bexar County Clerk by Juan E.

Barrera, Deputy; recorded May 16, 1901; Bk. 198, p. 26). Lien transferred to Morris Meyer of Williamson County, Tex., on March 3, 1904 . . . "Property free from liens except that given by us on Oct. 11, 1901 for $3000 to D. Hirsch. Said property not our homestead at time of lien on Oct. 11, 1901 (Bk. 225, p. 433+, March 3, 1904", in reference to 434 King William. On November 1, 1907 – G B Frank, as executor of Estate of Pauline Deutsch, transfers deeds to J. A. Hooper who refers to J. M. Nix and Birdie L. Nix having conveyed Lot 18 to J. A. Hooper for consideration of the sum of $2000 cash paid and the assumption by J. A. Hooper of the three last notes, two being for the sum of $1000 and one for $1500, the two prior notes, one for $500 and one for $1000, having been paid off and discharged by J. M. Nix and wife. Thus, the total amount of $5000 of notes represents the initial $4700 construction loan plus the 7% simple interest (not compounded). A summation of liens is herein referenced under notations 110 and 111.

58. Census records from 1910, 1920, and 1930 reflect renters who were bookkeepers, stenographers, salesmen, clerks, telephone operators, and engineers. During several periods of time, family groups were shown as renters as well as individual lodgers. Research conducted into this niche rental market suggests rooms for rent in the King William area around 1899 would have been leased for an estimated $20 per month.

59. Market research for room rentals, within single-family homes, in San Antonio at the turn of the century revealed rooms for let started around $10 to $12 per month in areas such as Monte Vista. King William would have commanded a higher rental fee due to its closer proximity to downtown businesses and rail stations in addition to its being a more fashionable neighborhood during the late nineteenth century. Comparative rents found in advertisement/classified sections of the *San Antonio Daily Express* reveals some pertinent data: (i) Rents had really not changed significantly from 1900 to 1907; (ii) Specific examples: "5 room cottage on Alamo Plaza - $30 monthly," "1910: 115 Magnolia – 5 rooms, modern $25.00 monthly," "East Quincy – 2 story residence - $35.00 monthly," "Laurel Heights – large modern dwelling - $50.00 monthly," "Denver Blvd – cottage $10.00 weekly," and "7 room house, all modern conveniences, will rent to right family." The majority of ads for houses or rooms for rent did not give the rental price nor the address. Finally, there was one ad in 1907 for a nice furnished room for rent at 102 Madison in the King William area; however, no rate was listed.

60. Financial proforma – Table 2.

61. Financial proforma – Table 1.

62. Real estate property taxes calculated into the financial proforma were researched for greater accuracy. San Antonio Public Library, Bexar County Tax Rolls, 1837-1910, Reels 7, 8, 9, 10, 11, 12.

63. "Twenty Five Years of Miracles," *The Mission*, Vol. 25, No. 1, Spring 1998. This anniversary publication and brochure of UTHSC at San Antonio states that in 1959 Governor Price Daniel signed House Bill 9, creating The University of Texas South Texas Medical School and that by 1965 the Nix Dairy Farm was conveyed to the State of Texas to build this great facility.

64. Matthews, Wilbur L., *History of San Antonio Medical Foundation and South Texas Medical Center.* "At that time the land now occupied by the Medical School and the other schools of the Health Science Center was the Joe J. Nix Dairy Farm, a wide expanse of grazing land, on which was located cattle pens, milking barns and two towering silos for storage of cattle feed. The transformation of the Nix Dairy Farm into a major medical center in a period of less than 20 years is, no doubt, San Antonio's greatest community accomplishment." p. 79.

65. Evett, Alice., *A Man . . . A Dream . . . A Company/The History of American Security Life Insurance Company.* "[. . . a group of prominent San Antonians formed] Five Oaks, Inc., and acquired a tract of land on the northwest side of the city. The group donated 25 acres as the future site of Southwest Texas Methodist Hospital which became the pioneer institution in the Medical Center. A further donation of 175 acres went to the non-profit Medical Foundation. The result has been the establishment of [the South Texas Medical Center]." p. 120.

IV. Building the Nix Houses

66. National Oceanic and Atmospheric Administration, United States Department of Commerce. Mean temperature for January 1900 was 48.5 degrees Fahrenheit. Representative of closest approximation of weather con-

ditions in South Texas for December 30, 1899. Information available online. See Internet Resources below.

67. Coote, p. 18. Coughlin and Atlee B. Ayres were in practice together in San Antonio from 1898 until Coughlin's death. Atlee B. Ayres (1873-1963), who studied architecture at the Metropolitan School of Architecture, housed within the Metropolitan Museum of Art in New York City, completed a full two-year course and received his diploma on May 26, 1894. Ayres was involved in more than 500 architectural projects including San Antonio's first sky-scraper, the Smith-Young Tower (now the Tower Life Building), the Atkinson house (now the Marion Koogler McNay Art Museum), San Antonio Municipal Auditorium, numerous private homes, businesses and churches and five buildings on the campus of the University of Texas at Austin. He was appointed Texas State architect in 1915 and had a professional career as an architect spanning 69 years.

68. Ayres, Atlee B., "Life with Father, An Autobiography," April 6, 1954.

69. Coote, p. 70.

70. Coote, p. 68.

71. "The American Architect and Building News," May 19, 1894, Vol. XLIV, p. 71, The American Architect and Building News Co., Boston, 1894. Avery Architectural and Fine Arts Library, Columbia University.

72. Howe, Winifred E. A History of The Metropolitan Museum of Art, p. 250.

73. Pine, John B., Charters, Acts of the Legislature, Official Documents, and Records, New York, Columbia University, 1920. Trustees' Minutes, Vol. XII, p. 53.

74. The Metropolitan Museum of Art Annual Reports, "Twenty-fourth Annual Report, Year Ending December 31, 1983." Annual meeting held on February 12, 1894, p. 574.

75. A handwritten letter of introduction dated May 1, 1893, by Met instruc-tor Seth Temple to Professor William Ware of Columbia College was an indi-

cation that Atlee B. Ayres was a highly regarded pupil at the school of art. One hundred years later, the author's professor, Kenneth Frampton, a noted British architect and architectural historian, was installed as Columbia's first Ware Professor of Architecture in honor of the same William Ware Ayres met. In an uncanny way, the author shares an historical path a century later: (i) Ware Professor Frampton offered a similar letter of introduction on behalf of Roy R. Pachecano, dated March 15, 1993, to architect Santiago Calatrava, and (ii) the author, like Ayres, returns to San Antonio from New York to design and develop the same corner in King William, (iii) both Ayres and Pachecano had British architects as early mentors.

76. Pachecano, Roy R. *MCMXCIII, Collection Work Completed at Columbia University.* Studio VI highlights work under British architect, critic Kenneth Frampton, Ware Professor of Architecture.

77. Demkin, Joseph A., Executive Editor. *The Architect's Handbook of Professional Practice*, Chapter I, Understanding Clients." written by Green, Kevin W. C., pp. 3-5. Much has changed in the regulatory activities of the practice of architecture. All architects practicing in the United States are state-licensed players in the building industry which is regulated by government and their participation, now mandated by law, serves as the primary regulatory device by which government ensures the preservation of life, safety, and welfare for the general public.

78. Sweet, Justin. *Legal Aspects of Architecture, Engineering, and the Construction Process*, p. 384.

79. "J. M. Nix - Contract with W. B. Massey with reference to Atlee B. Ayres," 30 Dec. 1899, Bexar County, Tex., Deed Book 185, pp. 608-609, Bexar County Courthouse, San Antonio, Tex.

80. The original drawings by Ayres' office do not exist. A full set of plans was redrawn by Portico Residential LLC in 2005.

81. Helen "Suzie" Brooks Piña stated she remembered hearing family members talk of the two houses being designed by the young Atlee B. Ayres.

82. Account books, 1899-1901, Coughlin & Ayres, Architects, Lockwood Bank Bldg, San Antonio, Tex.

83. Sweet, p. 115.

84. Sweet, p. 387.

85. The current dilemma facing the architectural community is how to revamp its schools and retool its future industry leaders to meet the increasing business, finance (including construction cost estimating, budgeting), and legal constraints each design project demands. As of this writing, few architectural schools in the United States embrace this pedagogical approach in favor of more esoteric, theory-laden design curriculum that few outside its circle understand.

V. Architectural Importance of the Nix Houses

86. Queen Victoria ruled from 1837 to 1901, an era marked by great social and technological changes, many of which had profound effects on the architectural development of the period.

87. Backer, Patricia Ryaby, "Industrialization of American Society." See Internet Resources below.

88. Trade catalogues in print from this period (1870-1920) offer much insight into the architecture, interior design, and domestic technology of the time. An extensive collection of such publications can be found at the Athenaeum of Philadelphia. One such reference is found in the decorative art pattern book entitled *H. Roessing's Excelsior Fresco & Stencils*, ca. 1918, copyright 1991 by the Athenaeum of Philadelphia. Other sample books prepared by medium-priced outlets were produced by Sears & Roebuck Company and Montgomery Ward—the latter a company built on a legacy that dates to 1872 when Aaron Montgomery Ward established the first mail-order business. The information gleaned from these sample books closely resembles the original wallpaper artifacts found embedded under layers of other wall coverings at the Nix Houses.

89. Osband, Linda, *Victorian House Style, An Architectural and Interior Design Souirce Book*, p. 8.

90. An ordinance reenacting Chapter 35, Unified Development Code, of the

City of San Antonio was passed and approved by City Council and Mayor Phil Hardberger on September 22, 2005.

91. Mandelker, Daniel R., and John M. Payne. *Planning and Control of Land Development: Cases and Materials*, p. 92.

92. New York City, Department of City Planning, Rezoning of East Harlem, December 16, 2002, is the date the Department of City Planning certified the Uniform Land Use Review Procedure (ULURP) application for the proposed zoning amendments. Approved by vote in Manhattan's Community Board 11 without conditions on February 18, 2003. The City Planning Commission held a public hearing on April 2, 2003, and voted to approve the proposal on May 7, 2003. On June 17, 2003, New York's City Council proposed a modification to the proposal by removing a midblock portion of land from the rezoning area. New York City Council adopted the proposal as modified on June 24, 2003. See Internet Resources below. http://www.nyc.gov/html/dcp/html/eastharlem/eastharlem1.shtml

93. Osband, Linda, *Victorian House Style*, p. 13. Almost $7^{1}/_{2}$ million newcomers entered the U.S. The third wave between 1881 and 1920 was the largest wave of immigration in the United States which changed how America viewed style.

94. Osband, p. 13.

95. American Face Brick Association, "The Home Fires." A trade publication devoted to proper fireplace construction.

96. Ohio Foundry & Manufacturing Co., Trade catalogue, brochure.

97. Dan Rottenberg's book, *In The Kingdom of Coal, An American Family and the Rock That Changed the World*, makes a compelling case of how anthracite not only changed domestic home heating but the greater United States economy during the late nineteenth and early twentieth centuries. His observations tie into one theme of this book: The growing national appetite for coal drove a nationwide obsession to develop railroad transportation capable of taking coal from mines to urban areas.

98. Aldine Manufacturing Co., "The Aldine Patent."

99. Romaine, Lawrence B. *American Trade Catalogs, A Guide, 1744-1900*, p. 25.

100. American Encaustic Tiling Co., Ltd., "Designs for Tile Pavements."

101. Barber, Edwin Atlee. *The Pottery and Porcelain of The United States*. Further study is available online at The Forum On Line Antiques Reference, "A Brief History of Ornamental Tiles in America." See Internet Resources below.

102. Hughes, Amy R. *This Old House: Joy of Vintage Tile*. 1993, This Old House Ventures. American Encaustic Tiling of Zanesville, Ohio, produced machine-pressed tile which was uniform thanks to smooth, purified ceramics and clays, crisp details, and a high-gloss glaze. The colors would range from dark amber to mint green with amethyst marbling and be made with a random pigmentation process that resulted in each piece of tile being unique. Thus, while mass-produced, each tile was highly unique and supported the late-Victorian decorative arts ideal of purity of individual craftsmanship while suppressing the sterility of mass production.

103. Wm. M. Taylor Mantel & Grate Co., Catalogue, 1900. Trade catalogues such as those produced by this company illustrate the refined manufacture of fireplace mantels in a variety of hardwoods. The firm would send its millwork through its offices in Chicago, Columbus, and Detroit.

104. Bailey, J. W., & Sons Co., Catalogue for Carpenters and Builders. Boston, Massachusetts, 1890.

105. McKinstry, Richard E. *Trade Catalogues at Winterthur — A Guide to the Literature of Merchandising, 1750-1980, A Winterthur Book*. p. 19.

106. Ostendorf, William G. *From Forest to Fireside*.

107. Manufacturing process of wood-pulp wallpaper was described by Gale Caskey Winkler, an authority on the decorative arts in the United States, who met the author at the Atheneaum of Philadelphia, November 10, 2006, in the institute's collections library in Philadelphia, Pennsylvania.

VI. Owners and Occupants of 432 and 434 King William

108. "Tired Commuters Fuel Teardown Trend," by Robert Weller, Associated Press wire, December 16, 2006. This article, which appeared in the *San Antonio Express-News*, cites the National Trust for Historic Preservation as claiming that "teardowns threaten the character of 300 communities in 33 states." This attitude towards demolition versus preservation varies from region to region but one thing remains clear: The debate will continue until an equitable, qualified, and fair balance in policy is achieved on how to deal with old and new structures, particularly structures found outside historic districts.

109. "J. M. Nix Designation of Homestead," July 31, 1903, Bexar County, Tex., Deed Book 222, p. 410, Bexar County Courthouse, San Antonio, Tex.

110. B. L. Nix to M. B. Gleason, "Release of lien," Bexar County, Tex. Deed Book 269, p. 497 and Book 534, p. 480-2, 1918; M. B. Gleason to J. M. and Birdie L. Nix, Bexar County, Tex. Deed Book 282, p. 401, Nov. 1, 1907. 432 King William was sold for $2,000 as partial payment for a tract of land of 1040 acres bought from Mary Beall Gleason of El Paso County, Texas. This acreage was used to establish the Nix Dairy Farm and was in the location now occupied by the University of Texas Health Science Center in San Antonio. A separate document transferred property on Houston Street from J. M. Nix to Birdie Nix "in consideration for her having deeded her [Birdie's] homestead on King William Street to M. B. Gleason. Mary Beall Gleason used the King William home as rental property. Mary Beall Gleason to May C. Hill, "Warranty Deed with Vendor's Lien, Bexar County, Tex. Deed Book 534, pp. 481-2 and Mary Beall Gleason and George D. Flory to May C. Hill, "Vendor's Lien Release", April 23, 1921, Bexar County, Tex. Deed Book 638, pp. 301-2, Bexar County Courthouse, San Antonio, Tex. Selling price was $3,500. May and Russell Hill to Virginia and Thomas C. Hardy, "Deed of Trust," Bexar County, Tex., Deed Book 813, pp. 589-590, May 23, 1921. Selling price was $3,000 in gold coins. Russell Hill and his partner, Wallace Rogers, are known to have been primary developers of the Monte Vista area in San Antonio. (See Donald E. Everett's book, *San Antonio's Monte Vista, Architecture and Society in a Gilded Age, 1890-1930.*) Virginia and Thomas C. Hardy had been renting the property for at least one year, if not more, prior to purchase. The U.S. Census, 1920, Bexar County, shows Thomas C. Hardy and wife, Virginia, as

renters at 432 King William. Virginia and Thomas Hardy sold by agent, Hazel Kaufmann, to A. W. and Edna L. Bouquet for $1,500 on Dec. 7, 1943. "Deed of Trust," Bexar County, Tex. Deed Book 2013, p. 263. The Bouquets transferred the property to their son A.W. Bouquet, Jr., "for love and affection" on Nov. 25, 1970. Bexar County Deed Book 7627, p. 839. On Dec. 12, 1991, A. W. Bouquet, Jr., deeded the property back to his mother, Edna Rose Bouquet, "Warranty Deed," Bexar County Deed Book 5219, p. 339, Bexar County Courthouse, San Antonio, Tex.

111. Mrs. Francisca Flores bought the 434 King William property from the Nixes in 1912 and lived there until around 1924. After her death in February 1944, the ownership of the property transferred to her great-niece and great-nephew, Maria Raquel Gutierrez and Luis Fernando Gutierrez. On March 5, 1946, the Gutierrez's sold the property to Rafael Lozano. "Warranty Deed to Rafael Lozano," Bexar County Deed Book 2203, pp. 601-607." "Estate of Luis Fernando Gutierrez, Minor – Guardian's Deed – Rafael Lozano." Rafael Lozano and Josefina Lozano soon sold the property on Oct. 14, 1946, to Maria Natalia de Arroyo and her husband, Cesar I. Arroyo, Bexar County Deed Book 2307, p. 593ff. The Arroyos sold to V. T. Garcia and Belen C. Garcia on Oct. 14, 1946, "Warranty Deed," Bexar County Deed Book 2423, p. 270ff. Then on May 27, 1948, the Garcia's sold the property to Mary Christine Carvajal. Bexar County Deed Book 2543, p. 147, Bexar County Courthouse, San Antonio, Tex.

112. "Warranty Deed with Vendor's Lien" from Mary Christine Carvajal Living Trust to Portico Residential, LLC, 15 Aug 2005, Bexar County, Tex., Deed Book 11586, p. 1499, Bexar County Courthouse, San Antonio, Tex.

113. Personal Interview conducted in San Antonio, Tex., on May 19, 2006, by Roy Pachecano with Alfonso Carvajal, brother of the late Mary Christine Carvajal.

114. Telephone interview conducted by Roy Pachecano on May 23, 2006, with Patricia Carvajal Tindall of San Marcos, Tex., niece of Mary Christine Carvajal.

VII. The Restoration Effort

115. *San Antonio Express News*, October 18, 2006. "Private Project Enhances Street," by Michelle Mondo. See Endnote 2.

116. As of this writing at the beginning of 2007, the City of San Antonio has not adopted green building guidelines for historic dwellings. Programs that are in place are only for new commercial and residential structures. The program "Build Green San Antonio" developed by the Metropolitan Partnership for Energy (MPE) and co-administered with the Greater San Antonio Builders Association has not written and adopted green guidelines for historic properties. MPE was created with the passage of Senate Bill 5 (SB5) by the 77th Texas Legislature and introduced a sweeping change in the state's approach to clean air and energy efficiency. The bill was enacted in 2001 to assist the State of Texas in complying with the federal Clean Air Act and contains new energy-efficiency measures for buildings that are designed to decrease energy consumption while improving air quality.

117. Frank J. Beitel was the son of Joseph (1806-1889) and Elizabeth Beitel (b? - d. Nov 1903). Joseph and Elizabeth were from Germany and arrived in San Antonio between 1830 and 1858. Joseph fought in the Battle of Plum Creek against the Comanches and the Battle of Salado against the Mexicans. In 1851, he purchased land on Salado Creek for $141.25 and began raising cattle. Joseph and Elizabeth had 11 children. Sons Frank and Albert went into the lumber business. According to Bexar County deed records found online, the lumber company was still entering into contracts as late as 1936.

118. As one example, in 1978 the U.S. Supreme Court set out to clarify its evaluation of historic buildings in light of what an owner is entitled, or not entitled, to do with its property. The high court's decision to hear a case involving an owner's desire to place a modern addition to its historic property essentially validated an economic principle (rather than an aesthetic principle) which has driven the manner in which all courts analyze a governmental "taking." In the landmark case *Penn Central v. City of New York*, the Supreme Court purposefully steered away from a ruling based on aesthetics. The lawyers arguing both sides of the case understood this and couched their respective arguments in terms of takings by a local government. The Court used an economic doctrine based on current and potential gains (investment-backed

expectations) the owner possessed when it appealed to the high court to allow it to build a modern skyscraper above its flagship Grand Central Terminal in midtown Manhattan. In the ruling, Penn Central was denied its right to build above its historic structure. Mandelker and Payne, *Planning and Control of Land Development*, pp. 101-114. Dowling, Timothy J., et al., "The Good News About Takings," p. 52.

VIII. Afterword

119. Freyfogle, Eric T. *The Land We Share: Private Property and the Common Good*, pp. 179-201. Eric T. Freyfogle earned his J.D. from University of Michigan, 1976, and has written numerous books on the topic of land use and property rights—everything from forest use to beaver dams to subdivision zoning—and uses the writing of classic property theorists and landmark legal cases to illuminate the ongoing debate about conflicts over private ownership and the greater accountability for those who misuse land.

120. Freyfogle, Eric T. "Land Use and the Study of Early American History," 94 Yale Law Journal.

121. Duany, Andres, with Elizabeth Plater-Zyberk and Jeff Speck, *Suburban Nation: The Rise of Sprawl and the Decline of the American Dream.*

122. Jackson, Kenneth, *Crabgrass Frontier, The Suburbanization of the United States.*

123. Gerckins, Lawrence. "Ten Failures that Shaped the 20th Century American City," Planning Commissioners Journal, Number 38, 2000.

Proforma Tables

THE NIX HOUSE AT 434 KING WILLIAM
BASE PROFORMA

	1899	1900	1901	1902	1903	1904	1905	1906	1907	1908	1909
YEAR	0	1	2	3	4	5	6	7	8	9	10
REVENUES											
POTENTIAL RENTAL REVENUE		$960	$970	$979	$989	$999	$1,009	$1,019	$1,029	$0	$0
CLEANING / LINENS		1	1	1	1	1	1	1	1	0	0
LATE FEES		5	5	5	5	5	5	5	5	0	0
TOTAL POTENTIAL REVENUE		966	976	985	995	1,005	1,015	1,025	1,036	0	0
LESS: VACANCY FACTOR		(242)	(68)	(69)	(70)	(70)	(71)	(72)	(72)	0	0
LESS: CREDIT LOSS		(7)	(9)	(9)	(9)	(9)	(9)	(10)	(10)	0	0
TOTAL		717	898	907	916	926	935	944	954	0	0
EXPENSES											
REAL ESTATE PROPERTY TAXES		(13)	(36)	(33)	(20)	(20)	(21)	(21)	(22)	0	0
OPERATING EXPENSES		(140)	(141)	(141)	(142)	(143)	(144)	(144)	(145)	0	0
MANAGEMENT FEE		(4)	(4)	(5)	(5)	(5)	(5)	(5)	(5)	0	0
TOTAL		(156)	(181)	(169)	(167)	(168)	(170)	(170)	(172)	0	0
NET OPERATING INCOME		561	717	738	750	758	765	774	782	0	0
CAPITAL EXPENDITURES											
RESERVE FOR REPLACEMENTS		(150)	(150)	(150)	(150)	(150)	(150)	(150)	(150)	0	0
LEASING COMMISSIONS A		0	0	0	0	0	0	0	0	0	0
TOTAL		(150)	(150)	(150)	(150)	(150)	(150)	(150)	(150)	0	0
NET CASH FLOW		411	567	588	600	608	615	624	632	0	0
MORTGAGE INTEREST		(167)	(167)	(167)	(167)	(167)	(167)	(167)	(167)	0	0
NET CASH AFTER DEBT		244	400	421	432	441	448	456	464	0	0
SALE											
UNDERWRITING CASH FLOW		0	0	0	0	0	0	0	790	0	0
CAP RATE		10.0%	10.0%	10.0%	10.0%	10.0%	10.0%	10.0%	10.0%	10.0%	10.0%
GROSS SALE PROCEEDS		0	0	0	0	0	0	0	7,903	0	0
SELLING COSTS		0	0	0	0	0	0	0	(119)	0	0
NET SALE PROCEEDS		0	0	0	0	0	0	0	7,784	0	0
DEBT REPAYMENT		0	0	0	0	0	0	0	(2,350)	0	0
NET SALE PROCEEDS AFTER DEBT		0	0	0	0	0	0	0	5,434	0	0
GRAND TOTAL NET CASH FLOW (UNLEVERAGED)	($3,600)	$411	$567	$588	$600	$608	$615	$624	$8,416	$0	$0
GRAND TOTAL NET CASH FLOW (LEVERAGED)	($1,250)	$244	$400	$421	$432	$441	$448	$456	$5,898	$0	$0

31. *Financial Base Proforma, 1899, 434 King William.*

LOAN ACCOUNT											
BALANCE BOY	0	2,350	2,350	2,350	2,350	2,350	2,350	2,350	2,350	0	0
PRINCIPAL BORROWED	2,350	0	0	0	0	0	0	0	0	0	0
INTEREST DUE @	7.12%	167	167	167	167	167	167	167	167	0	0
INTEREST PAID	0	(167)	(167)	(167)	(167)	(167)	(167)	(167)	(167)	0	0
PRINCIPAL PAYOFF	0	0	0	0	0	0	0	0	(2,350)	0	0
BALANCE EOY	2,350	2,350	2,350	2,350	2,350	2,350	2,350	2,350	0	0	0
SALE YEAR NOI CALC											
REVENUES											
POTENTIAL RENTAL REVENUE		$960	$970	$979	$989	$999	$1,009	$1,019	$1,029	$1,040	$1,050
CLEANING / LINENS							1	1	1	1	1
LATE FEES		5	5	5	5	5	5	5	5	5	5
TOTAL POTENTIAL REVENUE		966	976	985	995	1,005	1,015	1,025	1,036	1,046	1,056
LESS: VACANCY FACTOR		(242)	(68)	(69)	(70)	(70)	(71)	(72)	(72)	(73)	(74)
LESS: CREDIT LOSS		(7)	(9)	(9)	(9)	(9)	(9)	(10)	(10)	(10)	(10)
TOTAL		717	898	907	916	926	935	944	954	963	973
EXPENSES											
REAL ESTATE PROPERTY TAXES		(13)	(36)	(23)	(20)	(20)	(21)	(21)	(22)	(22)	(22)
OPERATING EXPENSES		(140)	(141)	(141)	(142)	(143)	(144)	(144)	(145)	(146)	(146)
MANAGEMENT FEE		(4)	(4)	(5)	(5)	(5)	(5)	(5)	(5)	(5)	(5)
TOTAL		(156)	(181)	(169)	(167)	(168)	(170)	(170)	(172)	(173)	(174)
NET OPERATING INCOME		561	717	738	750	758	765	774	782	790	799

1 Ad Valorem source: Bexar County Tax Rolls, 1837-1910, Reels 7, 8, 9,10,11,12

32. *Financial Base Proforma (continued)*, 1899, *434 King William*.

THE NIX HOUSE AT 434 KING WILLIAM
SUMMARY PROFORMA

YEAR	1899	1900	1901	1902	1903	1904	1905	1906	1907
		1	2	3	4	5	6	7	8
REVENUE		$717	$898	$907	$916	$926	$935	$944	$954
EXPENSE		(156)	(181)	(169)	(167)	(168)	(170)	(170)	(172)
NET OPERATING INCOME		561	717	738	750	758	765	774	782
CAPEX		(150)	(150)	(150)	(150)	(150)	(150)	(150)	(150)
NET CASH FLOW FROM OPERATIONS		411	567	588	600	608	615	624	632
NET SALE PROCEEDS		0	0	0	0	0	0	0	7,284
GRAND TOTAL NET CASH FLOW (UNLEVERAGED)	($3,600)	$411	$567	$588	$600	$608	$615	$624	$8,416
MORTGAGE INTEREST		($167)	($167)	($167)	($167)	($167)	($167)	($167)	($167)
PRINCIPAL REPAYMENT		0	0	0	0	0	0	0	(2,350)
GRAND TOTAL NET CASH FLOW (LEVERAGED)	($1,250)	$244	$400	$421	$432	$441	$448	$456	$5,898
YIELD ON COST		11.4%	15.8%	16.3%	16.7%	16.9%	17.1%	17.3%	233.8%
LEVERAGED YIELD		19.5%	32.0%	33.7%	34.6%	35.2%	35.8%	36.5%	471.9%
UNLEVERAGED IRR		22.0%							
LEVERAGED IRR		39.5%							

33. *Financial Summary Proforma, 1899, 434 King William.*

THE NIX HOUSE AT 434 KING WILLIAM
ASSUMPTIONS

LAND - PURCHASE PRICE (2 PARCELS)	$2,500	1 PARCEL	$1,250
LAND - EQUITY (2 PARCELS)	$1,800	1 PARCEL	$900
LAND - FINANCING (2 PARCELS)	$700	1 PARCEL	$350
CONSTRUCTION FUNDING (2 PARCELS)	$4,700	1 PARCEL	$2,350
CONSTRUCTION FUNDS FINANCING - 100% (2 PARC	$4,700	1 PARCEL	$2,350
DEVELOPMENT COSTS (LAND PP + CONSTRUCTION	$7,200	1 PARCEL	$3,600
BUILDING SF (PER)	2800		

ROOM RENTALS - 1 PARCEL	AREA (SF)	UNITS	RENT	REVENUE
1 B	150	1	$20	$20
2 B	150	1	$20	20
3 B	150	1	$20	20
4 B	150	1	$20	20
TOTAL	600	4		$80
AVERAGE	150		$20	

LOAN ASSUMPTIONS - 1 PARCEL

LOAN AMOUNT	$2,350	CHECK - VERIFIED
RATE	7%	
PAYABLE X PER YR	2	
APR EQUIVALENT	7.12%	

HOUSEHOLD LINENS (MONTHLY)	$1	FOR	5%
LATE FEES (MONTHLY)	$2	FOR	5%
VACANCY FACTOR (YEAR 1)			25%
VACANCY FACTOR (THEREAFTER)			7%
CREDIT LOSS			1%
REAL ESTATE PROPERTY T/ SOURCE: BEXAR COUNTY TAX ROLLS, 1837-1910, REELS			VARIED
OPERATING EXPENSES (PSF)			$0.05
OWNER FEE (% OF COLLECTED REVENUE)			1%
RESERVE FOR REPLACEMENTS (PSF)			$0.25
REVENUE GROWTH RATE			1.0%
EXPENSE GROWTH RATE			0.5%
RENEWAL RATE			25%
YEAR OF SALE			8
CAP RATE ON SALE			10.0%
SELLING COSTS			1.5%

	YEAR 1	YEAR 2	YEAR 3	YEAR 4	YEAR 5	YEAR 6
LEASING COMMISSIONS (NO	0%	0%	0%	0%	0%	0%

[1] *This amount was discharged before construction completion. Nix's total equity raised to $1,250.*

[2] *Each dwelling, $3,600 less equity of $1,250 = $2,350*

[3] *Modern capitalization rates would not have been used in the original deal structure.*
It is incorporated to analyze the 1899 development using contemporary modeling techniques.

34. *Financial Proforma - Assumptions, 1899, 434 King William.*

Bibliography

Books

Allen, Paula, *San Antonio, Then and Now,* San Diego, Calif, Thunder Bay Press, 2005.

Appler, Jules A. *General Directory and Blue Book, City of San Antonio,* 1896, 1901-1902, 1903-1904.

Ayres, Atlee B., "Life with Father, An Autobiography," April 6, 1954, Atlee B. Ayres Collection, Institute of Texan Cultures Archives, San Antonio, Tex.

Bailey, Ernest Emory, *Texas Historical and Biographical Record, With a Genealogical Study of Historical Family Records,* Austin, Tex.., The Texas Historical and Biographical Record, n.d.

Barber, Edwin Atlee, *The Pottery and Porcelain of The United States,* 2d Ed., NY, G. P. Putnam's Sons, 1902.

Brockman, John Martin. *Railroads, Radicals and Democrats: A Study in Texas Politics,* 1865-1900. Dissertation, University of Texas at Austin, 1975.

Brueggeman, William B., and Fisher, Jeffrey D. *Real Estate Finance and Investments,* Eleventh Edition, NY, McGraw-Hill, 2001.

Buenger, Walter L. *The Path To A Modern South: Northeast Texas between Reconstruction and the Great Depression.* University of Texas Press, Austin, Tex., 2001.

Burkholder, Mary V. *Down the Acequia Madre in the King William Historic District.* Privately printed, 1976.

Burkholder, Mary V. and Graham B. Knight. *The King William Area, a History and Guide to the Houses.* San Antonio, Outland Press, 1977.

Coote, Robert James. *The Eclectic Odyssey of Atlee B. Ayres, Architect.* Color Photographs by W. Eugene George. College Station, Texas A&M University Press, 2001.

Coughlin & Ayres, Architects, Lockwood Bank Building, San Antonio. *Ledgers,* 1899-1901. On loan by Ayres family member to Tom Shelton, Photo Archivist, Institute of Texan Cultures, San Antonio.

Demkin, Joseph A., Executive Editor. *The Architect's Handbook of Professional Practice.* John Wiley & Sons, Inc., for The American Institute of Architects, 2001.

Dowling, Timothy J., Kendall, Douglas T., Bradley, Jennifer, "The Good News About Takings", The Citizen's Planning Series, The American Planning Association, Washington, D.C., 2006, p. 52.

Duany, Andres, Elizabeth Plater-Zyberk and Jeff Speck, *Suburban Nation: The Rise of Sprawl and the Decline of the American Dream.* NY, North Point Press, 2001.

Everett, Donald. *San Antonio's Monte Vista: Architecture and Society in a Gilded Age, 1890-1930.* San Antonio, Maverick Publishing Co., 1999.

Evett, Alice. *A Man . . . A Dream . . . A Company / The History of American Security Life Insurance Company,* 1981, San Antonio.

Fisher, Lewis F. *Riverwalk, The Epic Story of San Antonio's River.* San Antonio, Maverick Publishing Company, 2007.

Freyfogle, Eric T. "Land Use and the Study of Early American History," 94 Yale Law Journal, the Yale law Journal Company, Inc., 1985.

Freyfogle, Eric T. *The Land We Share: Private Property and the Common Good.* Washington, D.C., Island Press, 2003.

Gerckins, Lawrence. "Ten Failures that Shaped the 20th Century American City," Published by Planning Commissioners Journal, Number 38, 2000.

Green, David P. *Place Names of San Antonio plus Bexar and Surrounding Counties.* San

Antonio, Maverick Publishing Co., 2002.

Hemphill, Hugh. *The Railroads of San Antonio and South Central Texas.* San Antonio, Maverick Publishing Co., 2006.

Howe, Winifred E. *A History of The Metropolitan Museum of Art.* The Metropolitan Museum of Art, New York, 1912.

Jackson, Kenneth. *Crabgrass Frontier, The Suburbanization of the United States.* 1987, Oxford University.

Lich, Glenn E. *The German Texans.* San Antonio, University of Texas Institute of Texan Cultures at San Antonio, 1981; revised, 1996.

Livingston, James. *Pragmatism and The Political Economy of Cultural Revolution, 1850-1940.* University of North Carolina Press, Chapel Hill, 1994.

McKinstry, Richard E. *Trade Catalogues at Winterthur—A Guide to the Literature of Merchandising, 1750-1980, A Winterthur Book.* New York, Garland Publishing, Inc., 1984.

Mandelker, Daniel R., and Payne, John M. *Planning and Control of Land Development: Cases and Materials.* Fifth Ed. LexisNexis, Matthew Bender & Co., Inc., 2001.

Matthews, Wilbur L. *History of San Antonio Medical Foundation and South Texas Medical Center,* 1983, San Antonio.

Norton, Chas. G., ed. *Men of Affairs of San Antonio.* San Antonio Newspaper Artists Association, [1912].

Osband, Linda. *Victorian House Style: An Architectural and Interior Design Source Book.* London, David & Charles Publisher, 1998.

31. Pachecano, Roy R. *MCMXCIII, Collection Work Completed at Columbia University.* Limited edition, Printed by The International House of New York, 1993.

Pine, John B., *Charters, Acts of the Legislature, Official Documents, and Records,* New York, Columbia University, 1920.

Romaine, Lawrence B. *American Trade Catalogs, A Guide, 1744-1900*. New York, R. R. Bowker Company, 1960.

Rottenberg, Dan. In *The Kingdom of Coal, An American Family and the Rock That Changed the World*. Published by Routledge (an imprint of the Taylor & Francis Group) 2003.

Rust, Joe Carroll. *Historic Bexar County, An Illustrated History*. Bexar County Historical Commission, Historical Publishing Network, Lammert, Inc., 2006.

Schmidt, F. A. "Rails to the Artesian Belt," Vertical Files, Barker Texas History Center, University of Texas at Austin, 1977.

Sweet, Justin. *Legal Aspects of Architects, Engineering, and the Construction Process*. Fourth Edition, 1989. West Publishing Company, St. Paul, Minn.

Trade Catalogues/Professional Periodicals, Brochures

Aldine Manufacturing Co., "The Aldine Patent," Grand Rapids Michigan, 1890. Avery Index Trade Catalogues, Avery Architectural and Fine Arts Library, Columbia University.

"The American Architect and Building News," January-March 1893, Vol. XXXIX. May 19, 1894, Vol. XLIV. Boston, Ticknor & Co. Avery Index Trade Catalogues, Avery Architectural and Fine Arts Library, Columbia University.

American Encaustic Tiling Co., Ltd., "Designs for Tile Pavements," 1900. Department for Drawings and Prints, The Metropolitan Museum of Art, New York.

American Face Brick Association, "The Home Fires," Chicago, 1925. Clearwater Publishing. Avery Index Trade Catalogues, Avery Architectural and Fine Arts Library, Columbia University.

Bailey, J. W., & Sons Co., "Catalogue for Carpenters and Builders." Boston, Mass., 1890.

"Twenty Five Years of Miracles," *The Mission*, Vol. 25, No. I, Spring 1998, Office of Public Affairs, University of Texas Health Science Center, San Antonio.

Ohio Foundry & Manufacturing Co., Trade catalog, brochure. Steubenville, Ohio, 1900. Department for Drawings and Prints, The Metropolitan Museum of Art, New York.

Ostendorf, William G., From Forest to Fireside. C. B. Atkin, 1903. Avery Index Trade Catalogues, Avery Architectural and Fine Arts Library, Columbia University.

"Wallpaper Samples – A Book of Beautiful Decorating Possibilities." Montgomery Ward & Co., New York, 1910. The Athenaeum of Philadelphia, Athena Online Catalogue. See internet reference below.

Sample Book of Wallpaper, Sears & Roebuck Company, Chicago, 1905. The Athenaeum of Philadelphia, Athena Online Catalogue. See internet reference below.

Wm. M. Taylor Mantel & Grate Co., Catalogue, company brochure. Chicago, 1900. Avery Index Trade Catalogues, Avery Architectural and Fine Arts Library, Columbia University.

Internet Sources

The Athenaeum of Philadelphia, Athena Online Catalogue. Architectural drawings and decorative arts research library. http://www.philaathenaeum.org/catalog.html

Backer, Patricia Ryaby, "Industrialization of American Society," San Jose State University, College of Engineering, San Jose, Calif. http://www.engr.sjsu.edu/pabacker/industrial.htm

Bexar County Appraisal District website: Bexar County Appraisal District, True Automation, Inc. http://www.bcad.org/

Bexar County Clerk's Office, online access to Bexar County deed books. Landata Technologies, Inc., 2006. http://www.countyclerk.bexar.landata.com/

City-Data.com, online San Antonio historical information compiled from the San Antonio Conservation Society. http://www.city-data.com/us-cities/The-South/San-Antonio-History.html

The Forum On Line Antiques Reference, "A Brief History of Ornamental Tiles in America," http://www.the-forum.com/pottery/tiles.htm

Federal Reserve Archival System for Economic Research (FRASER), Annual Statistical Digest. http://fraser.stlouisfed.org/publications/astatdig/

Hughes, Amy R. *This Old House: Joy of Vintage Tile.* 1993, This Old House Ventures. http://www.thisoldhouse.com/toh/print/ 0,17071,1084935,00.html

Handbook of Texas Online website, Texas State Historical Association. http://www.tsha.utexas.edu/handbook/online/articles/SS/hjs18.html

Long, Christopher, "King William Historic District," in Handbook of Texas Online, http://www.tsha.utexas.edu/handbook/online/

National Oceanic and Atmospheric Administration, United States Department of Commerce. http://climvis.ncdc.noaa.gov/cgi-bin/cag3/state-map-display.pl

New York City, Department of City Planning website. http://www.nyc.gov/html/dcp/html/eastharlem/eastharlem1.shtml

ProQuest Information and Learning Company, University Microfilms. http://proquest.com/brand/umi.shtml

Texas General Land Office website. http://www.glo.state.tx.us/ archives/land-grant.html.

Texas Transportation Museum, The Longhorn Chapter, The M-K-T (Missouri-Kansas-Texas) Depot and History. http://www.txtransportationmuseum.org/MKTB.htm

Texas State Data Center, Institute for Demographic and Socioeconomic Research University of Texas at San Antonio http://txsdc.utsa.edu/tpepp/2005_txpopest_county.php

U.S. Census reports, 1880 from the National Archives, Washington, D.C. provided by the Family History Library, Church of Jesus Christ of Latter Day Saints, Salt Lake City, Utah, 1993-2005, Intellectual Reserve Inc., http://www.familysearch.org/

U.S. Census reports from the National Archives, Washington D.C., provided by the Texas State Library through the TexShare Databases accessing Heritage Quest Online. http:// www.heritagequestonline.com/prod/genealogy/index

Wikipedia, A Free Encyclopedia, Wikimedia Foundation. http://en.wikipedia.org/wiki/Main_Page

Interviews

Alfonso Carvajal, brother of the late Mary Christine Carvajal. Personal interview conducted by Roy Pachecano on 5/19/2006 in San Antonio, Tex.

Alfonso Carvajal of San Antonio, Tex. Telephone interview by Patricia Ezell on 5/24/06, San Antonio, Tex.

Helen "Suzie" Brooks Pin?a, daughter of Josephine Nix Brooks and David Brooks, great-granddaughter of Birdie Lanier Nix and J. M. Nix. Telephone interview conducted by Roy Pachecano on 4/18/2006, San Antonio, Tex.

Christopher D. Ross, son of Helen Brooks Pin?a, grandson of Josephine Nix Brooks and David Brooks, great-grandson of Birdie Lanier Nix and J. M. Nix. Telephone interview conducted by Roy Pachecano on 4/20/2006, San Antonio, Tex.

Christopher D. Ross. Telephone interview conducted by Patricia Ezell on 5/22/2006, San Antonio, Tex.

Patricia Carvajal Tindall, of San Marcos, Tex, niece of Mary Christine Carvajal and daughter of Alfonso Carvajal. Telephone interview conducted by Roy Pachecano on 4/23/2006, San Antonio, Tex.

Robert James Coote of Austin, Texas. Personal interview conducted by Roy Pachecano on 11/13/2006.

Personal interviews with Katie Coiner Parks, Helen "Suzie" Brooks Pin?a and Christopher D. Ross conducted by Patricia Ezell and Roy Pachecano on 11/29/2006.

Newspapers

The Light, San Antonio, Tex., June 1, 1932, Microfilm roll, San Antonio Public Library, Texana/Genealogy Department.

The San Antonio Express, San Antonio, Tex., June 1, 1932, Microfilm roll, San Antonio Public Library, Texana/Genealogy Department.

San Antonio Daily Express, San Antonio, Tex., March 2, 1907, Microfilm roll, San Antonio Public Library, Texana/Genealogy Department.

San Antonio Express-News, San Antonio, Tex., December 16, 2006. "Tired Commuters Fuel Teardown Trend," by Robert Weller.

San Antonio Express News, San Antonio, Tex., October 18, 2006. "Private Project Enhances Street," by Michelle Mondo.

ABOUT THE AUTHOR

Roy R. Pachecano has had his hand in design and construction ever since he was a boy walking construction sites with his father. With over 20 years of professional experience, Mr. Pachecano has enjoyed working in all facets of the real estate development industry and has practiced in all major aspects of development itself: design, construction, finance, law, and politics. A developer, Mr. Pachecano is also a trained and licensed architect. His twin companies, Portico Residential LLC, and Portico Real Estate Investments LLC ("Portico REI") are based in New York where he has represented major corporations, institutions and private clients in the proactive practice of real estate development. The firms were created to advise on and reposition unique, distressed properties.

Mr. Pachecano's consulting career began when he co-founded the Design Consulting Department with Barry B. LePatner, Esq., within his nationally recognized law firm located in New York City. In addition to serving clients who are some of the world's most prestigious institutions, corporations and multi-national banks, Mr. Pachecano has had the honor and privilege working with some of the best attorneys in the industry.

Portico Residential and Portico REI were incubated while attending Columbia University's Real Estate Development program in 2003. Mr. Pachecano combined his studies in real estate development by cross registering with the university's Urban Planning, Architecture, Business and Law schools adding to his broad experience attained in the professional world of zoning, land use law, and financial and physical asset due diligence reporting. Mr. Pachecano has overseen pre-transactional due diligence volume worth over $500 million comprised of new and historic properties. Fluent in the review of all design, construction, finance, market, legal, asset management and physical plant conditions that inform market valuation, Mr. Pachecano's success in consulting has greatly aided him in his successful private development projects.

Mr. Pachecano has written and published numerous industry-related articles and has been featured and/or appeared in the New York Times, Architecture Magazine, PBS' Ask This Old House, and Home and Garden Television (HGTV). He currently teaches at Pratt Institute's Center for Continuing and Professional Studies at its Manhattan campus on topics affecting real property: zoning/land use and real estate development.

Photo by Annette Hernandez

THE NIX HOUSES

COLOPHON

This book is set in 11-point Centaur type

on #70 Williamsburg offset paper with 80# Rainbow endpapers.

Book Design by Fishead Design Studio.

Printing by Litho Press, Inc. Binding by Universal Bookbindery.

THE
WATERCRESS
PRESS

San Antonio, Texas